Out of the Blue Into the Black

The autobiography of John Spencer

The Parrs Wood Press
Manchester

First Published 2005

THE PARRS WOOD PRESS
St Wilfrid's Enterprise Centre
Royce Road, Manchester, M15 5BJ
www.parrswoodpress.com

ISBN: 1 903158 63 X

Printed and bound by Biddles Ltd of King's Lynn

To Jean

Contents

Acknowledgements

There are many people I would like to thank, not just for the help in writing this book, but for help and support throughout my life. Firstly, my father, for making arrangements for me to be able to go down The Grott on my own (you'll understand as you read on!). Les Taylor, for coming to see if I would play for his team when he didn't know I hadn't touched my cue for 11 years. Margot, for helping me early in my career when finances were tight and having faith in me. Nick Hunter at the BBC, for giving me the chance to commentate, which kept me involved in snooker after Myasthenia Gravis shortened my career. Jean, Margot, Peter Dennis, Clive Everton, Jim Wych and Roger Lee for their help with the book. Ted Lowe for all his help during the drafting of this book and the foreword. Sindhu Pulsirivong, my spiritual brother, who has always been there when I needed him. Steve Annable of the Myasthenia Gravis Association. David Clayton for making sense of my writing and Andrew Searle at Parrs Wood Press for his belief and support with the book.

Foreword

THIS BOOK portrays the wicked sense of humour of a snooker champion whose brilliant potting, break-building and studious tactical play awarded him three world titles.

Born in Radcliffe in 1935, just outside Manchester, John took up the cue at the age of 15 and within a short period of a couple of years compiled his first snooker century. However, National Service intervened and he put his cue away for a few years. In that time he found work in a bookmaker's office, a love and interest he still enjoys today. To gamble with him at snooker, golf or cards could prove foolhardy.

The green baize beckoned again in 1964 when he entered the English Amateur Championship and won his way through to the final. It was there he met and lost to the player with whom he was to share the next decade at the very top of professional snooker, Welshman Ray Reardon. Between them they won nine world professional snooker titles, Reardon taking six to John's three.

For 20 years John Spencer was a force to be reckoned with; in addition to his world titles, his many other triumphs included three Pot Black victories (1970, 1971 and 1976). Unfortunately his health began causing problems in the mid-Eighties. It started with a disease that caused double vision, professionally fatal to a world-class snooker star. Treatments brought further complications, though he returned to the scene in 1985 but finally put his cue away in its case for the last time in 1990.

OUT OF THE BLUE INTO THE BLACK

The fun-loving Spencer, however, never lost his sense of humour. Having fought against cancer (and other illnesses) with the help of his partner Jean, he relates for you in the pages of this book some of the antics, leg-pulls and mischievous gags he performed on those around him.

I know I was on the receiving end of many of them!

Ted Lowe, July 2005

Chapter 1

Out of the Blue

Pontin's 1985

THE WORST day of my life was May 9, 1985. I was at Pontin's Holiday Camp, Prestatyn, playing in a tournament when all of a sudden I felt really tired, which I put down to nothing more than having too much to drink the night before. I decided to go back to my chalet and have a lie down. I will always remember the time as it is etched in my memory... it was 2.50pm when I lay down on the bed for a nap to recharge my batteries; if it was a hangover as I suspected, I'd sleep it off. But it wasn't the booze on this occasion though it would still be a while before that sank in. I woke up at 4pm and I could see two of everything wherever I looked. It scared me to death. Within a few minutes everything was back to normal so it seemed perhaps it was a touch too much alcohol the previous evening.

Little did I know what effect this incident would have on me soon after and later in life.

At about 7pm that same day, I set off on my way home when I suddenly saw two white lines in the road. One of the lines was stretching up to the sky so I pulled in to the side of the road and had a short rest. Eventually it cleared up again and I finally managed to get home. This situation went on for a couple of weeks;

sometimes the double vision lasted minutes, other times it lasted for an hour.

A while later, I decided to go with three of my mates for a game of golf at Regent Park Golf Club in Bolton. When I arrived at the first tee and stood over the ball it seemed to start moving around and I knew something was wrong. Feeling totally frustrated and not a little unnerved by what was happening, I immediately picked up my ball and said I would see them in the clubhouse when they had finished. I got myself a cup of coffee and sat near the window of the 18th green. While I was looking out of the window two identically dressed golfers came onto the green about five yards apart. They were heading for one ball on the green and one ball in the bunker a few yards away. When they both putted out simultaneously I knew that there was something drastically wrong with me.

Of course, by the time my mates had finished their round of golf everything was back to normal so I didn't say anything to them as they would have thought I was off my rocker, but as soon as I got home I phoned a specialist and made an appointment to see him at the earliest convenience, which, fortunately, turned out to be the day after. He said it sounded like it could be one of three things; it could be diabetes, an aneurysm or Myasthenia Gravis. This really scared me as my father had died of an aneurysm, so he did a few tests and then said he wanted me in hospital within three hours so that he could do further investigations. I really bottled it then. I was in the Manchester Northern Hospital within the hour and had to stay in for three days while they did about 30 different tests, all of which at least ruled out diabetes.

OUT OF THE BLUE

During my time in the hospital one of the male nurses, who was absolutely snooker-mad, kept coming and chatting to me about the game, which I was happy to do, but I obviously had more pressing matters on my mind. I was questioning him about the diseases and I finished up lying there trying to decide which I would prefer it to be. I decided that I would settle for the Myasthenia Gravis, so when they finally told me that that was what it was, in a perverse way I suppose I was quite happy. Had I had any inkling as to the problems I would have to face with the disease in the future, I doubt I would have felt as relieved as I did. It was a very rare condition in those days - in fact, when I went to see my own doctor he had never heard of it.

The specialist then sent me to see a neurologist, who asked me when my next snooker tournament was. I told him it was in September and he said he would try and get it cleared up by then but he would have to put me on a high dose of steroids, which could have side effects. He also told me that he did not know whether I had the ocular version of the disease or whether it would spread throughout all the muscles in my body and that they wouldn't be able to tell me either way for at least twelve months. I was scared to death - every time I felt a twinge in any part of my body I was convinced it was the Myasthenia Gravis spreading.

As it turned out I was one of the lucky ones, if anyone with Myasthenia Gravis can be classed as 'lucky', as it turned out to be the ocular version, so I just had the side effects of the steroids to worry about. But that was bad enough as they brought on a massive bout of depression. Though I had double vision, the strange thing was that if I put a patch over either eye I could see clearly out of the other. Then, about two months later, I was sat in the office of my good mate Vince Laverty, a local newspaper owner, and was looking out of the window when I suddenly started to shout out the names of the shops on the opposite side of the road. As I had not got my patch on, Vince realised the double vision had gone and a lot of my depression seemed to dissipate immediately. The neurologist had done his job; he had just got rid of the double vision in time for me to play in the first tournament of the season, which was the Scottish Masters in which I lost on the pink to Silvino Francisco.

It then took the neurologist two years to reduce my dosage of steroids down to two tablets a day. With this reduction in my treatment, my double vision returned so he had to up the dosage again to 10 and 5 on alternate days, then reduce them over the next month until he got me down to three a day. With this the double vision cleared again and that is the dosage I am still on to this day. When the double vision does break out occasionally I have to immediately up the steroid intake again and the whole cycle has to begin again until it has cleared up. In an unfortunate twist of fate, the neurologist who had treated me has now got Myasthenia Gravis all through his body. Aristotle Onassis was another person who died from it. A few years ago I got a telephone call from Channel 4 TV asking me if I would appear on a programme about Myasthenia Gravis, as two people who they knew had committed suicide rather than continue to suffer from it. Not really what you want to hear, is it? For some reason I never heard anything else about it but I could sympathise with the poor souls who'd decided enough was enough.

I wasn't going to join them, however.

Chapter 2

Back to the Beginning

Radcliffe 1935-1948

I WAS born on September 18, 1935 in Radcliffe, a small industrial town on the outskirts of Manchester. I was the youngest of five children with two older brothers, Peter and Bobby, and two older sisters, Joyce and Edna. Being the youngest child, I was very close to my mother and always was until the day she died.

There were seven of us living in a three-bedroom council house when I was a boy. I suppose we were a rather poor family but we never seemed to want for anything as we were very happy and close-knit, held together mainly by my mother. My father was a war veteran and had lost his right arm during the First World War. I always remember him telling me that they should have amputated it above his elbow but they would only amputate below it so he couldn't claim as much pension as he should have been entitled to and he was always in a lot of pain because of this. One thing I remember about my father was that although he couldn't work much, he was always a very smart man, often wearing a trilby, shirt and tie.

My father wasn't able to get a regular job due to his handicap so he became a night watchman at a local factory and also a bookie's runner. Only having one arm never seemed to hamper him too much as he could do all the necessary jobs around the house. I don't know how but he managed to build a shed complete with shelves so that there was somewhere to store everything. He also built a fabulous greenhouse that he made entirely of old picture frames, which he'd collected from either people who were throwing them away or some he would find on rubbish tips. It took him quite a long time to build this but he managed it in the end and it looked magnificent, you would have thought that professional tradesmen had built it. He also would paint and decorate our house using only one hand and he would not let any of us help him.

All the neighbours were fantastic with us. When Christmas came we never went short of Christmas presents, some of which I found out later had been given to us by our generous neighbours. One of the things I most remember about this time was that on Christmas Eve, the Radcliffe Borough Brass Band always arrived outside our house at midnight on the dot and played my father's favourite carol, *Silent Night*. All the neighbours came to their doors and sang along with the band, which always brought tears to everyones' eyes, including my father's. When they had finished, all the neighbours shouted and cheered. It was a humbling, warm time.

One of the most memorable moments of living in Radcliffe during the war years was when a Doodlebug bomb overshot its intended target of Manchester and fell just one mile away from our house on the outskirts of our neighbourhood. It caused quite a stir, as everyone wanted to see where it had landed. Thankfully no one was injured by it.

OUT OF THE BLUE INTO THE BLACK

In 1946 I sat and successfully passed the entry exam for the local Grammar school. However, I was a little embarrassed as it meant that my mother and father had to find more money to buy me a uniform to attend Stand Grammar. Despite this, they still managed it and never once complained about the cost. My very first bet on the horses was when I was a pupil at Stand Grammar School. I looked in the daily paper when I arrived home from school and saw a horse running the following day called Étoile Glissant. I had just finished a French lesson that day, which had mentioned that this name translated from French into 'shining brightly', and there was another horse called Xavier, which happened to be the name of the comic I was reading. Armed with such insider info, how could I lose? I told my father about these omens and he put a shilling double on for me. Would you believe that they both came home winners and I won 2 shillings and 10d? That was my first foray into gambling, but was not to be my last.

With money scarce, sometimes there were nine of us in our three-bedroom council house. This was because my two elder sisters and two elder brothers had their fiancés stay when they were home on leave from their National Service in the army. I used to have a single bed in the front bedroom with my mother and father in a double bed, but many a time if one of my brothers came home unexpectedly I would have to move in with my mother and father. Some nights when a friend might stay we had to put a form at the side of the bed and sleep across the bed, but somebody always seemed to kick the form over and leave five pairs of feet sticking out. There was also a mad dash in the morning to get in the bathroom first, and for the record I was always the last one in. Every two weeks, the whole family would set off to Darwen to see my Grandma (my dad's mum) who was very religious, so we had to be very careful what we said. We would just sit there at the table waiting for our tea and would have to say grace before our meal. We were always relieved when it was time to go home. The journey itself was not an easy one as we didn't have a car and would have to travel by bus, which would take us about three hours one way.

It was also about this time that Aubrey Jones, who was the Conservative Party candidate for our council house estate and its strongly Labour-supporting people, was making a speech for which a small crowd had gathered. When he got on to the subject of rationing and how the Conservatives would provide more eggs for everyone, my sister Edna, who was never one for holding back, shouted, "Why? Can Aubrey Jones lay eggs?" and everyone just burst out laughing. That was the last we saw of Aubrey Jones.

When I was fifteen years old I went down Radcliffe to the local 'Bop' shop where everyone used to meet for a drink - soft drinks only, of course. I met one of my friends, Ronnie Parker, whose dad owned Bluebird Motor Coaches in Oldham. He was going for a ride in one of his dad's coaches and asked me if I wanted to go with him so I said yes. We set off and ended up near Radcliffe Paper Mill Clubhouse at about 11 o'clock at night, on a dirt road. Someone must have seen us and become suspicious, wondering what a coach was doing down there at that time of night, and notified the police. They duly arrived to investigate any potential crime and Ronnie told me to just tell them we had been to the 'floating lights' near Morecambe. They came on board and found a stash of lead that had been stolen, which Ronnie was planning on delivering to someone on that estate. They took us down to the police station to interview us both. I was frightened about what my mother may think I had been up to, but once in the police station Ronnie told the police that I had nothing to do with it. He said he had just invited me to have a ride in his coach and convinced them that I was unaware about the lead stash. To my relief they let me go. I got home in the early hours of the morning, where my mother was waiting for me, worried sick and I had to explain the events of the evening to her.

Chapter 3

Early Breaks

Manchester 1948-1953

I WAS introduced to snooker for the first time when I was thirteen. My older brother Bobby used to go round to his friend Donald Fairbanks' house for a game of snooker, so one day I decided to follow him there. When I got there they wouldn't let me in so I went round to the side of the house and sat on the garden wall to watch them play through the window. I don't know what the fascination with the game was but there was certainly something about it that kept me going back every week just to sit outside and watch them. Little did I know what this burgeoning fascination with the game would lead to in the future.

Shortly after this Bobby turned up one night with a Bagatelle Table, which was about four foot by two foot with a polished top and green baize on the bottom. When it was opened up I saw that it had nine cups at one end with a snooker-type cushion behind them, the idea being that the cups were numbered 1-9 and you had to score as many as possible by getting the balls in the cups. Eventually we got the idea of turning the table upside down so that the green baize was on top. We then knocked nails in the corners and the centres as pockets and then tied a lot of tape round and round these nails to act as the cushions. The cushions, to our surprise, worked pretty well as long as you didn't hit them too hard; if you did then the ball just rolled over the top of the tape and on to the floor. I spent many a happy hour playing on this makeshift table.

By the age of fourteen, my father, who had seen how much I was enjoying the game, surprised me when he asked if I would like to go to the local billiard hall in the centre of Radcliffe, which was called The Grott. This was situated under the market place in the cellar where the River Irwell ran alongside. Its location meant that sometimes, during very wet weather, the river would rise and flood the billiard hall. Once we were inside The Grott and we had reached the snooker table, I wondered how my father was going to play snooker with just the one arm. I should have known better than to question his ingenuity. He then pulled out of his inside pocket a small clothes brush. He used this to slide the cue along the top of its bristles until he lined the ball up, then he would just push the cue down into the bristles and use it as a rest. I couldn't believe what I was seeing when he started with a 23 break! Later, as we were leaving, he had a word with the man behind the counter and arranged for me to be able to go and play down there on my own. Tom, the manager, agreed to this even though you should have been 18 years old to play alone - as long as I played on a table in the corner. I could not believe that all this was happening and couldn't wait to get down there on my own.

From then on I went down to The Grott every day that I could find the time and it was here I met a local bookmaker called Les Taylor who, as it turned out, was destined to become one of the biggest influences on my life - I used to play against him five days a week for two or three hours at a time at both billiards and snooker. After a while, I started playing some of the other members for a shilling a frame, which became very profitable for me. After that, I virtually lived down The Grott and made my first 100-plus break when I was just fifteen. I will always remember it because it started with a red and a yellow, then 14 reds and fourteen blacks, which made a 115 break. After that I started making century breaks regularly.

One day I was playing a man called Bill Holt who used to come in to the club quite often. I was winning our game by five frames, for a prize of a shilling a frame, when he gave me his cue and said, "Hold this while I go to the toilet," which was upstairs in the market place. I had been sat waiting there for about five minutes when a very good friend of mine, Dougie Cooper, came in and saw me sitting there holding the two cues. Dougie said, "I bet you're playing Bill Holt and he has gone to the toilet." I said he was right and Dougie told me to go and pay for the table, as Bill wouldn't be coming back; apparently he had done this to Dougie as well, so I had to go and pay for the table and never got my five shillings. It was not long after this that my father died of an aneurysm. I was grateful to him for taking me along to The Grott as he had got me started playing snooker seriously and for that I am eternally indebted to him.

After losing my father there was only my sisters, my mum and myself at home as my older brothers were away doing their National Service. I have to say that I think my mother may have spoiled me as she would make a drink for me, put in the sugar and stir it for me before bringing it to where I was sitting. In fact she did everything for me. I just took all this in my stride and thought it was natural, but it caused a few problems later in life when I got married and had to do them all for myself. I lost count of the number of times that my mother sent me shopping and, instead of going straight home with the shopping, I would call into The Grott to play, frequently leaving the shopping there when I left. I would have to run back down to The Grott after being told off by my mother for going in there instead of going straight home. But I couldn't help myself - it was like a magnet to me and try as I might (not very hard I admit), I just couldn't pass it and it virtually became my second home. There is one thing I remember about going shopping for my mother; I went round to the local shop, which was called Nellie Smith's, for the groceries and on the list there was always a packet of 'Happy Days' and I was 16 years old before I found out that they were in fact sanitary towels. That was obviously my mother's own code for them!

I was also very keen on cricket at this time and played for the Stand Grammar's Under-14s. I also practised at Radcliffe Cricket Club. They had always had one of the top overseas professionals who came over and played for them, such as Sir Frank Worrell, Sir Garfield Sobers and Cec Pepper. They also used to have coaching sessions a couple of nights a week - I always turned up there for this coaching and thought at that time that I would like to become a professional cricketer.

EARLY BREAKS

Tom, the manager of The Grott, sold me a cue which had the number 35 burnt into the shaft. People could hire these cues for one shilling a year to play snooker, but were not allowed to take them out of the billiard hall. However, he said I could take mine out as I had bought it. All it cost me was 8 shillings and even though it was bent like a bow and had a nail in the bottom of it to hold it together, it was the cue with which I won the first two World Championships.

I enjoyed playing so much that I started going to the local Church Institute where a friend I knew played and they let me become a member. I finished up playing for them in the local league and made quite a big name for myself around the town. The local newspaper, the *Bury Times*, used to run a handicap around the Radcliffe and Bury clubs and they decided to ask me if I would go round these various clubs and play a three-frame match against whoever had won that particular night. This turned out to be terrific for me, as the winner who had to play me was obviously scared of losing to a 15-year-old, whereas I just couldn't wait to get on the table.

It wasn't long before I was playing in front of full houses in these clubs and the next thing there was an article and photograph of me in the *Bury Times* with the heading 'Boy snooker player with a big future'. I went to school the next day and at about 11 o'clock, Mr Medler, the headmaster, sent for me. It was the first time that I rushed to his office, thinking he was going to congratulate me about the photograph in the paper; instead, he gave me the biggest talking to that I ever had and warned me what would happen if I let snooker interfere with my homework. Medler by name...

OUT OF THE BLUE INTO THE BLACK

Soon after, it was arranged for me, still aged just 16, to play Joe Davis at Holdsworth Hall, where all the professional snooker players played their matches when in Manchester. I'll never forget the evening as the table was one of the most ornate I had ever seen. The cushions on the table did not stop at the pockets, the woodwork was carved around each pocket and it was a new experience to play on such a grand table. When I got in on the black, due to the speed at which I was moving round the table I nearly broke my hip on the woodcarvings around the pockets. It was not a match as such; I was there just so he could see me play. It was going to be arranged for me to play him again but for some reason this never came off. For a 16-year-old to play Joe Davis, the World Champion, was a dream come true.

I decided not to sit the grammar school leaver's exam and left when I was 15 so that I could bring a bit more money in for my mother. From the age of 15 till 18 years old, I had seven different jobs, which were quite varied. I found it hard to settle in any one job, as all I wanted to do was play snooker. I started off as an accountancy clerk at Joe Morris's in Radcliffe, then at the General Electric Company (GEC) as an apprentice engineer, a cost clerk at Bibby and Baron's paper mill, a labourer at Fletcher's Paper Mill as well as being a debt collection clerk in Manchester, sending out threatening letters to people. The one I most remember was being an apprentice motor mechanic at a local garage, which I was really enjoying until my mother made me leave after three weeks because I was getting my hands dirty. My mother did this because she thought I needed nice hands to play snooker. Perhaps she had a point and it proved just how much my family believed in me.

All the jobs I had were in Radcliffe and as near to The Grott as possible so that I could spend my lunchtimes playing snooker, which, as things turned out, did not do me any harm. I went as a raincoat cutter to Solar Wear, a garment factory which was just down the road from The Grott, so I was playing snooker every lunchtime and many a time I was late getting back into work. Eventually Brian, the manager, sent for me and warned me what would happen if I was late anymore. I then told him, politely, to "Stick your job up your arse as I can earn more in a day playing snooker than you're paying me for a week," and with that I got my coat and walked out. Unbeknown to me, my sister Joyce went for a job at the same place about a month later and of course she mentioned to him that her brother had worked there. He said, "Yes, I got to know him very well," and told her what I had said, but he still gave her the job so no harm was done on my part!

Chapter 4

Flying Without Wings

RAF 1953-56

IN 1953 it was time for me to do my National Service, but instead I decided to join the RAF for three years instead of the regulation two years. You got 21 shillings a week more and an extra three weeks' leave, a month off at the end of your three years for you to find a job to go to when you were discharged, and a far better chance of promotion.

I will never forget my first day in the RAF, as we had to go to Cardington to get kitted out. We were given quite a number of forms to fill in, which were then collected by the sergeant about five minutes later. He came back out into the hall and bellowed, "Have we got a John Spencer in here?" So I stood up, wondering what I had done. He then asked me to go up on to the stage, for what I did not know, and he then turned to the rest of the recruits and shouted, "We have a right one here. Would you believe that this person here does not know when he was born, what sort of start is that?" Everyone in the room burst out laughing. He then turned to me and showed me my Birth Certificate which said '15th September 1935', and I had put down '18th September 1935'. Apparently what had happened was that my father when he registered me had put his mother's birthdate on the birth certificate by mistake. It had gone unnoticed until I joined the RAF so even now, although I celebrate my birthday on the 18th, I still have to fill any official forms in as 15th September 1935. So it was not a good start to my first day in the RAF.

I was sent to West Kirby on the Wirral to do my three months squarebashing and as I was 6ft tall I got various duties that needed someone with height. One of these was sentry duty, in which I had to stand in the sentry box at the main gate and if the Wing Commander or any other officer passed in his car you had to take two steps forward and salute him by presenting arms. Sure enough, within half an hour I saw his car coming round to the gates so I immediately presented arms, then took two steps forward only to find that the rifle had not come with me. Of course, I had forgotten to take two steps forward before I presented arms and all he saw was me trying to pull the bayonet out of the sentry box roof. It must have happened regularly as the Wing Commander was laughing his head off as he went past and the roof of the sentry box was full of bayonet marks.

Another time we were on 'Night Patrol', which meant you had to go round the camp every two hours checking that all the buildings on the site were locked. On our second tour we found that the door of a big office was not locked but we were scared of going in. We must have stood there for about five minutes wondering what to do before we decided not to bother about it. We were walking away when the Sergeant's voice screamed out at us from inside the building, as he was testing us to see how we did our job. He put us on a charge the next day. Still, I have always been a coward. I was also a marker when we were marching and everyone had to line up behind me.

I was still in West Kirby over the Christmas period so a friend and me decided to go to the local dance hall and have a few drinks. We soon got chatting to these four girls and were getting on really well with them when this little bloke came in and started to chat to them as well. As he was only about 5ft tall and I was 6ft I had a chance to show off in front of the girls, so I threatened to take him outside as I accused him of trying to muscle in on our girls. He agreed to do this, so off we went outside and that was all I remember as he turned out to be the RAF amateur boxing champion - I was never off the floor. It taught me a lesson I'd never forget and I have never willingly been near a fight since.

I finished up at Compton Bassett near Calne in Wiltshire and luckily there was a corporal in the billet from Radcliffe who had a car, so I was able to get home nearly every weekend, which made my mother a lot happier. The first time we went out to a pub in Calne the locals could tell we were sproggs (new recruits) and they all wanted to buy us a pint of scrumpy, which apparently was rough cider and only cost 8d a pint. As most of the customers were drinking it we thought we'd join in as well. All I can say is that it tasted like sour vinegar, it was horrible at first, but it was amazing how quick you acquired the taste for it. We just about managed to get through two pints and we were all nearly drunk. I was at Calne for the whole of my three years but try as I might, I could never get through three pints of the bloody stuff in a night. Still, it was a cheap night out at 8d a pint.

FLYING WITHOUT WINGS

I had to go to Hereford on a couple of courses, one of which was to become a corporal. I managed to pass this course but did not get my promotion for another six months as the Wing Commander did not think I was capable of being in charge of a company of men as he thought I had no leadership qualities. I am sure that he was right, as on one occasion the Sergeant ordered me to tell the rest of the men in my billet to polish the floors, but when I tried to tell them they just laughed and said do it yourself, which I ended up doing so that I would not be on a charge the following day! The trouble was that I had been living with all these in the billets since I went to Compton Bassett and they were all pals of mine, so when they wanted a laugh they made me do the floor polishing. When eventually I was given my corporal's stripes, I got about 6 months back-pay, which was from when I had passed the corporal's test in Hereford - needless to say that I finished up pretty drunk that night. I was eventually put in charge of the barracks store and every Thursday we would have a clothing parade where the WRAFs got kitted out. Well, you can imagine the fun we used to have with "What size are you?", "What colour do you want?" and the "Let me have a look" that was the WRAF clothing parade; anything for a laugh.

I was also picked to play cricket for the RAF at the Trowbridge County Ground and I cannot tell you how big that ground looked; the walk from the pavilion seemed enormous. Would you believe that I managed to run the Wing Commander out and, after scoring a single in the next over, I was clean bowled myself? I can assure you it is a long walk back to the pavilion on those county grounds, especially when you have just run the Wing Commander out. I could not understand why but I was never picked again, not even for the camp team.

Eventually I was demobbed on November 16th 1956, but we had a night out for me leaving and I got so drunk on a cocktail of drinks and I didn't get home until the 19th. In fact, on the morning of the 17th I had a cup of tea in the barracks and felt as though I was drunk again, so I ended up sleeping on the mattresses in the barracks store with my mates bringing food in for me until I was able to go home. Still, all in all, the time I spent in the forces certainly did me a lot of good; it certainly made me appreciate things that I used to take for granted. Incidentally, though I was in the RAF for all this time, I never actually saw an aeroplane in all the time I was there!

Chapter 5

Hustle and Bustle

1956-1964

WHEN I left the forces I had taken on various jobs and again found it difficult to stay in any one of them, just as I had done before my time in the RAF. I first went into an accountant's office, but the job only lasted about three weeks as I got bored being on my own all day and having no one to chat to, although at school my favourite subject had always been Maths.

My next job was as a driver for Abe Tobias' Jewish bakery, delivering the pretzels and bagels to all the Jewish shops in the Manchester area. I promise you, working for a Jewish bakery was the most unusual job I ever had. I had to be there at 5am to load the van up and have all the deliveries finished by 7am. I was always on time with the bagels, but every shopkeeper screamed and shouted at me when I arrived, saying I had cost them money because I was late.

Then it finally happened. One day I was in Cheadle with Abe, the governor of the bakery, when we started arguing about something and nothing. He told me to get out and get something from the back of the van that he wanted to show me, but as soon as I got out he drove off, leaving me stuck in the middle of Cheadle, a good seven miles from work, at 7 o'clock in the morning. I had to walk back to the bakery, managing to thumb a lift after I had walked about three miles, but I was very careful never to argue with him again.

I then finished up working for his son Derek who had opened a betting shop in Radcliffe. I worked as a settler and without a doubt that job suited me better than any other as I had always liked to have a flutter myself on the horses and football. I also became the only non-Jewish member of the Jewish Workingmen's Club in Prestwich and used to spend quite a lot of time in there, although it was only open in the afternoons. I just loved to have a game of kalooki and there was always plenty in there that wanted to play. Over the time that I went in there, I think that I made a profit as well as making a lot of friends.

The longest job I had during this period was at the Radcliffe paper mill where I was an oiler and greaser, and my partner in crime at the paper mill was a Ralph Sherlock. As we had to do some shift work we had to work during the holidays and some weekends, too. We had to go round all the machinery and clean, oil and grease every part of it. The beauty of this, of course, was that we were on double time throughout these periods and there were many times when we had nothing to do at all except sit in our cabin. About four of us used to work together and go out for a pint afterwards and one Christmas lunchtime we went for a few drinks to the British Queen pub on Stand Lane, Radcliffe, which was the nearest pub to the paper mill. We must have got carried away when the landlord, Ernie Monaghan, said to us "It's 3 o'clock now, closing time," but instead of just going home we decided to stay there. Ernie said we must go down in to the cellar so no one would know we were drinking after time, so we stayed there drinking straight from the barrel. At opening time in the evening he came down the cellar and said, "You can come up now, it's legal, it's opening time," so up we went and carried on for another session. When I got home I went to the bathroom, and that is were my mother found me later on, fast asleep in the bath in all my work clothes, though she did not wake me and decided to let me sleep it off.

It was not long after this that my mother and me moved house into a prefab on Wordsworth Avenue in Radcliffe. This was one of the best houses that we lived in, as everything seemed to be in the right place. They should have only been up for 15 years but by the time we moved out they had been up for 30 years. It was here that I decided to have a go at decorating the prefab but as I had never had to do anything like that before I made a bit of a mess of it, so our Peter and my brother-in-law Norman came up and decorated it for us.

It was while I was working at Lonsdale & Thompson's Warehouse as a wages clerk that I had a visit at home from Les Taylor, who I used to play snooker and billiards with every day before I went in the forces. He still thought that I was playing snooker but I had not touched my cue since I was 18 years old and eleven years had passed. He told me that there was a snooker match between Longsight and Salford snooker clubs, who played against each other every Sunday for £5 a head, and his team had got beaten nine weeks running. He had told the manager that he would bring a player who would beat any player in either of the teams, thinking that I was still playing, so he came to my home and told me what had happened. I told him that I had not played snooker for some years but decided, after a lot of thought, that I could not let him down and I would attend on the following Sunday. Little did I know that this decision would change my life forever and steer me in a new direction.

So I went to the cupboard to get my cue out from where it had stood for a number of years. As soon as I opened the cupboard door and reached in to get it, my father's false arm, a great heavy leather thing, fell out and nearly broke my foot. I then picked up my cue, which was absolutely covered in dust; were it not for Les Taylor coming to see me that day I am sure my cue would still be in that cupboard now. I have often thought what I would have done had he not come to our house that day. It certainly made me a great believer in what will be will be. With the match coming up, I began to visit St Mary's Social Club in my lunch hour for half an hour's practice each day and I must confess, I played a lot better than I thought I would after an 11-year lay-off.

I arrived at the Longsight Club on the Sunday evening and sure enough I was marked down to play last. The fact that the rest of the team thought that there was a Joe Davis playing for them had inspired them so much that they were 65 in front when it was my turn to play, which just goes to show the confidence it gave them. It was also a relief to me to start with a lead - if we had been level I think that I would have lost as I was very nervous while I was watching the other games before mine. Of course, going on 65 points in front gave me the confidence that

I needed. My opponent was the top amateur in Lancashire at that time, a man called Austin Whiteside. Having seen him play, I asked Les to see if he could fix me up with some money matches as I was sure I could make some money out of playing snooker if his game was the top standard in the Lancashire area. I then started playing money matches against all the top players around the Lancashire area. I lost my first match against Stan Holden 4-3 at Radcliffe Social Club, but that was the only one that I lost so I made quite a nice profit. This initial success in my local games had also got me thinking of entering the English Amateur Championship.

I was working as a stacker in MacPherson's paint factory when one of my mates came up to me and said he had entered me into a snooker handicap at Walshaw Conservative Club. I was off a 14 start and a bookmaker was laying me at odds of 6 to 1. However, they could re-handicap after the first round so I had to make sure that I did not make any big breaks or win my first match too easily. Anyway, we went up to play and I made sure that I did not win by too many in the first round. Then we put our bets on and after this I could not be re-handicapped. I then won the next round without any problem before making a century break to win the semi-final. It was quite funny when the bookmaker came over to us and paid us out our winnings before we had even played the final round. He said that was the first time he had been taken in like that and he would make sure it would never happen again.

It was at this time that I did all my playing in the Bolton Billiard Hall along with Stan Holden and Doug French. We were asked if we would sign on for

OUT OF THE BLUE INTO THE BLACK

Wavertree Labour Club in the Liverpool League and decided that we would, driving to Liverpool every Monday night to play for them. The difference between the two leagues was tremendous; instead of a crowd of about 20-30 people watching the matches, like in the Bolton League, we would get crowds of over 200 people, all shouting and cheering throughout the matches, wherever we were playing. Against their biggest rivals, which was Walton Trades and Labour, there must have been getting on for 250 people in the crowd, which made for a tremendous atmosphere.

The first time we played them at home I was put down to play George Scott, who was the champion of Liverpool. When I beat him by quite a large margin, the cheering just went on and on. Another night we set off driving for Merseyside in a fog that had become a pea souper before we arrived, so Stan Holden said he would get out and walk in front of the car until it cleared a little. Whilst doing this, we came to an underpass and that was the last we saw of Stan Holden that night - don't ask me where he ended up!

One day a hustler arrived called Blackpool Danny, who used to come to the Bolton Billiard Hall to earn his 'wages'. It was the first time I had seen him but I had heard a lot about him. He used to play various members of the club for a couple of shillings and would let them win the first two or three frames, and then he would win the rest of the match. This would go on all day until he ran out of people to play that hadn't already been hustled by him. One day I was in the billiard hall while he was there and Stan Holden arranged for me to play him. We started playing off level and it finished up that I was giving him a 25 start at the end and still beating him. Eventually he gave up the ghost and said he would not be playing me again, no matter what start I would give him, as I had taken him to the cleaners. This was obviously the first time that had ever happened to him and I never saw him again.

I also used to go to the Bolton Greyhound Track on a regular basis with a pal of mine, Willis Blackshaw, who was a bookie's runner there. I lost count of the number of times we had to walk home as we had lost all of our money on the last race. Some years later I actually bought a share in a greyhound along with Willis and three other people, which we called Charlie's Lad, and a friend of mine Geoff Charlton, whose nickname was 'Charlie', used to take it on so people didn't know whose dog it was. It was a good greyhound and nearly won first time out. It was supposed to be stopped, to raise the price for the next time it went out, but needless to say it won by a distance so was not worth backing at the odds given for the next time it ran, which meant the early end of my greyhound ownership.

Chapter 6

Around the World
in 80 Plays

Amateur Championship 1964-1966

I FIRST entered the Amateur Championship in 1964, the first year it had been split into two regional sections: the Northern Amateur Championship and the Southern Amateur Championship. The two winners would meet in the final at Central Hall, Birmingham, which was a Methodist Mission Hall. I won the Northern section very comfortably, which meant that I would have to play Ray Reardon the following month as he had won the Southern Amateur Championship. It was a close run match as we were level at 7 frames all, but Ray managed to beat me over the final five frames to win 11-8.

The Methodist Mission Hall had no-smoking signs all over the place but, as I'd always smoked when I played snooker, after a few minutes of play I got out my cigarettes and lit one up. About five minutes later, it looked like Bonfire Night as all the spectators got their cigarettes out and started to smoke. This incident was picked up by the *Daily Mirror* who ran a small piece about it in the paper the following day, which had the headline: 'John Spencer Causes A

Touch of the Andy Capp'. Well, not quite, but old habits die hard.

Another exhibition I played in was at Leigh Conservative Club, where I had taken Julie, my girlfriend at that time, along with me. When I got there they told me it was a men only club and they said that Julie could not come in. So I said, "I am not playing unless Julie is allowed to stay and watch the snooker." The committee members called a meeting and said that Julie could stay in the lounge part of the pub. I said that unless she could watch the snooker I was not playing, as I had not been told about this situation before I came. If I had I would not have brought her with me so the next thing the committee held another meeting and it was decided that we should go to the Anchor Cables Social Club, which was a quarter of a mile down the road, and play the match there. Suddenly the committee, Julie, myself and about 100 spectators all descended upon this club, which was virtually empty and only had one man behind the bar who was sat reading the paper. He looked astonished when we all walked in. I managed to win the match comfortably so I was quite happy with the move, although I do not think the man behind the bar was too happy as he had to phone round to get some more staff in to cope with the crowd.

When I reached the final of the Amateur Championships, Harold Phillips, the chairman of the Billiards and Snooker Association, had obviously never heard of me as it was the first time that I had entered and I got a letter from him asking me to send a photograph as soon as possible. The only photographs I had were holiday snaps and, as I didn't know anything about publicity, I just picked out the one with me, my mother and my brother Bobby in swimming trunks outside Scarborough baths, put it in an envelope and sent it off to Harold Phillips. I would love to have been a fly on the office wall when Harold Phillips opened the envelope as I found out later that he was a bit of a snob. However, about three weeks later the *Billiards and Snooker* magazine dropped through our letterbox at home and on the front page it showed two photos, one of Ray Reardon in a suit, waistcoat and tie and the one of me, my mother and brother in swimming trunks outside Scarborough baths. Underneath the caption under the photo it said, "John Spencer is the right hand member of the group of three, the other being Mrs Spencer and his brother Bobby."

I again reached the final of the English Amateur Championship in 1965 and lost in the final to Patsy Houlihan, 11-3, at Blackpool Tower. I probably played worse in that final than any other tournament that I had ever played in and all I could put it down to was thinking that it was going to be easy as I was a big odds-on favourite to win. Consequently, my over-confidence led to me not putting enough practice in, though this defeat taught me a good lesson and I never went into another tournament with that attitude. I started to put more practice in than I had ever done before.

It obviously did me a lot of good in hindsight as I won the English Amateur Championship in 1966, beating Marcus Owen by 11-5, and set up a record by making the first century break ever in the final. This meant that I would have to go to Pakistan to play in the World Amateur Championship, which would mean having my first flight and my first trip overseas. When I got to Heathrow Airport I just could not wait for them to call us on board to see what it was like when the plane took off. I was thrilled to bits when it finally happened, but little did I know that within one year I would be sick to death of flying.

When I got there and was taken to the Muslim Gymkhana, which was the venue for the Championship, I was very impressed with the seating and the area round the table. It was a first class venue. I was then taken to the house where I would be staying and I got the shock of my life when I was told that I was staying with a multi-millionaire called Noorali Fancy, who owned Crockfords Casino in London as well as about twenty different companies in Pakistan and was also the Chairman of the Pakistan Snooker Association.

On the first morning that I was there he asked me what I would like for breakfast. I said I would have a couple of boiled eggs and some toast as I only liked English food and spicy food would upset my stomach. The following morning when I went for breakfast I could not believe what I saw. There was a full English breakfast waiting for me and apparently what he had done was to get the first British Airways flight into Pakistan in the morning to deliver a full English breakfast to his house for me and that went on for the three weeks that I was there. I just could not imagine the cost of that but it certainly did not do me any harm. I enjoyed every breakfast that I had and when I went for a cigarette after breakfast a bearer would shoot from behind a curtain with a lighter and light my cigarette for me. There was just nothing you could do without one of the bearers appearing - even when I went for a shower the bearer would be there to wash me down - it was simply amazing. Noorali Fancy also provided me with a chauffeur-driven car for the whole of my visit. While I was there I had made friends with another snooker player called Bert Demarco who came from Edinburgh. As he had not had any transport provided for him I invited him to come with me to the tournament in my chauffeur-driven car and we have remained friends ever since. During my three-week stay there the only Pakistani word I ever learned was "Atcha" which must mean OK, as that was the only word we got out of my driver. Whatever we said to my driver, all he ever said was "Atcha".

The championship itself was played in a round-robin format with six players including myself, Gary Owen, Mohammed Lafir of Sri Lanka, Bill Barrie of Australia, Bert Demarco of Scotland and Hamed Karim of Pakistan. The round-robin format suited me down to the ground and I could not believe the standard of play. I went on and eventually finished second to Gary Owen. I was also proved right with not having Indian food, as I was the only one not to go down with a bad stomach. Whilst in the country, Gary Owen, Mohammed Lafir, Bert Demarco and myself also had a visit to East Pakistan and played exhibitions at Dacca and Chittagong.

The strangest result I had as an amateur was when I played Dennis Robertson on ITV in the best of three frames. I just managed to win 2-1 when they found out the cameras had broken down so we had to play the match again. This time I lost the match 2-1! The trouble with the amateur matches was that if it was the best of three frames, then you had to make sure that it went to 1-1. If it was the best of five frames then it had to be 2-2, so it actually paid you to lose the first two frames so you then had the next two frames to find your form. I think that shows what the governing body for the amateurs knew about promoting snooker to the nation. There was an inquiry later regarding this set-up with ITV promoting a false image of snooker.

It was at this time that I was approached by the National Spastics Society, who used to have a few professionals who went round the country playing exhibition matches on their behalf and raising money for charity. They offered me £14 per night plus a small commission on the amount I raised, with a raffle and an auction of snooker cues and presents that the audience had brought for the charity. They said they would arrange all the shows and of course pay all my expenses. It surprised me the number of shows that they got me playing at as I was only expecting the odd one or two a week. On the first week that I started to play on their behalf I had five shows, all around the Middlesbrough area, so I spent my first week playing another professional called Jackie Rea, who was also playing for the Spastics Society. He taught me in that one week how to entertain people and get them laughing and of course how to make them laugh when showing them the trick shots.

The first night I did the trick shots they went down better than I thought they would, as I was very nervous - not having done them before in front of a full house. The next night, Jackie Rea told me to change the order in which I did the shots and it was amazing the difference this made to the crowd. They went down so much better, probably like a comedian telling his jokes in a certain order. I remember there was one particular trick shot that I did which was to put a red over the baulk pocket, put the white on the baulk line, then hit the white onto the black cushion. Then, when it came back, I hit it on the bottom so that it went back towards the black cushion, before the spin I had put on it brought it back and potted the red. When one fellow in the audience said he didn't understand what I meant, without thinking I told him I hit it once and then again, and with that the crowd were in uproar for a few minutes before I finally played the shot. So after that, when I got to this particular shot and I had explained what I was going to do, I always asked the audience if they all understood. There was always someone in the crowd who asked if I would explain it again and without a doubt it became by far my best trick shot for getting laughs.

In 1967 I had an idea that as you did not get many exhibitions in the summer I could play an exhibition and do some trick shots at one of the Pontin's holiday camps. So I went to see the manager, Bill Armistead, about doing these at their Blackpool holiday camp and after a lot of thought he said he would give it a try and offered to pay me £20 per week. It was about this time that I started seeing a woman who worked for the RAC in a caravan on the edge of Bolton Bus Station. I used to go and meet her there and we would go and have a drink in the White Lion pub, which was just on the corner. The barmaid there wore the shortest mini-skirt I'd ever seen, which, by pure coincidence, was when I started drinking bottles of lager as they were on the bottom shelf - I admit I just loved to see her bend down in that mini-skirt. She was called Margot and although I was pretty sure she knew what I was doing it certainly did not bother her. One night we were talking and I mentioned that I had a week of exhibitions in Bournemouth and Margot said that was where her mother and father lived. If I gave her a lift to Bournemouth she would let me stay at her mother's and father's house instead of having to pay for a hotel. So we decided to do this and spent a week together down there, but little did I know that this would eventually lead to us getting married.

I will always remember the very first exhibition that I played as a professional. I had arranged this exhibition before I turned pro, which was at the Troy Street Pensioners' Club in Blackburn for £3. I was the first amateur to turn professional since 1951 and as soon as this became known, the secretary Jack Tomlinson was on the phone to me to see how much more it was going to cost them now. I told him the price would remain the same as he had booked me when I was an amateur. When I went to play this exhibition I did not know what to expect, but I must say it was one of the best receptions I have ever had as everyone stood up applauding. When he came to pay me at the end of the evening I said, "Just give me a packet of cigarettes," - which he did. It was not long before I got a lovely letter from Jack inviting me to play there again the following year. So once again I was going into the club to a standing ovation and Jack was there to greet me. He took me for a cup of tea and we were having a chat when he said to me, "Do you remember Jimmy Birch who you played third last year? He was very unlucky. He was 24 in front in the final of the Christmas Handicap when he had a heart attack and later died from this." I don't know how I stopped laughing, as they were not concerned that he had dropped dead but that he had done it when he was in front in the Christmas Handicap. But I must confess as I have got older I have understood a lot more, that at a large Pensioners' Club like Troy Street, members dying was a much more regular thing than the average club.

Talk about a coincidence, in March 1969 I was playing an exhibition at Southsea Conservative Club with Joyce Gardner, the lady professional, and during the interval I got chatting with this couple and their daughter. After I had finished the exhibition I had a few drinks with them and eventually they invited me back to their house for a few more drinks. During the conversation I said that I was spending the summer season at Pontin's holiday camp giving exhibitions and later on they said that I could stay the night, as I was not fit to drive after all I had drunk throughout the evening. I thanked them for their hospitality and after breakfast the following morning I set off on my way home and thought no more about them. In May of that year the couple's daughter and her friend went to the Pontin's Holiday Camp at Blackpool for a week's holiday and as they were checking in they asked the receptionist there if John Spencer was on the camp. But the receptionist they had asked happened to be Margot, the girl with the short mini-skirts who worked behind the bar in Bolton and who I had started courting. She asked them how they knew me and she said, "Oh he stayed at my house whilst in Southsea earlier this year." I had to try and explain to Margot what had happened and that it was all innocent. Whether she believed me or not, I don't know, but she never mentioned it again.

The exhibitions I had played at Pontin's were a success and always packed to capacity so the management decided to stage two tournaments at Prestatyn every year during the month of May, which was then thought of as the end of the snooker season. The first one was the Pontin's Professional and I finished runner-up, losing in the final to Ray Reardon by the odd frame in 19. The same week saw the Pontin's Open, which was contested by both amateur and professional players, and, with it being the end of the season for exhibitions, they got more entries than they ever expected. The first of these was played in 1974 and I got to the final of the Open, losing by 7 frames to 4 to Doug Mountjoy. The following year I again got to the final of the professional tournament and was beaten rather easily. In 1977 I finally managed to win the Pontin's Professional Tournament and in 1978 I was again runner up in the Professional Tournament. I must say that these competitions did a lot for the game of snooker as every match was guaranteed a full house of spectators and the atmosphere was terrific to play in. As well as those watching, it also encouraged a lot of youngsters to take up the game, as this was also when the new style of first-class snooker clubs started opening all over the country, which had originally started with the *Pot Black* series on BBC television.

OUT OF THE BLUE INTO THE BLACK

The winner of the Pontin's snooker tournament won the privilege of playing a special match with me, which was over three frames. Each week players would enter and it was run on a knockout basis. Besides the match with me, the winner would also win a Joe Davis snooker cue and a free weekend at the camp. It was such a success that Bill Armistead then asked me if I would include Morecambe, Southport and Prestatyn holiday camps in my itinerary and he would make it £50 per week plus free accommodation at their camps. So there was money coming in all the year round for doing something I loved. I don't think that there is a better feeling than being able to entertain people and especially to be able to make them laugh.

I arrived at the Blackpool camp one day, just as the assistant manager was leaving. He said he was going to Blackpool Airport for flying lessons and would I like to go along with him as his guest. I said yes and the next thing I knew I was sitting in a little aeroplane with the instructor, the assistant manager and myself. We were eventually airborne when the plane turned right and started to descend. When I looked I could see the runway in front of us, though he didn't land the plane and instead suddenly zoomed off back up into the sky, which made me wonder what was happening. He did this six times by which time I was panicking as I thought he didn't know how to land the plane. I can assure you that this was the only time that I actually panicked in a plane but the next time he landed without any problem. It seems he was just being taught how to approach the runway and not to land; nevertheless it was the most frightening thing that has ever happened to me in an aeroplane.

One of the first Bluecoats that I had bumped into at Morecambe Bay Holiday Camp in 1968 was Margot, whom I had met previously in Bolton (unbeknown to me she had got a job there). This is when Margot and I started courting seriously before we were married on April 5th, 1969 at Bury Register Office. As I had been booked by Rileys Snooker to go to Bermuda for two weeks of exhibitions, we arranged for Margot to come out for the second week, which would be our honeymoon. The person responsible for booking this was Will Minors, a black man who had opened a few sports stores around the island, and this was going to be a promotion for the company.

The first morning Will came to the hotel and took me on a tour round the island, showing me all the beautiful places to go and visit. It amazed me that the speed limit was just 20 miles per hour and nobody ever seemed to exceed it. The sand on the beach was actually pink, it is truly a beautiful island and I don't think I have ever been anywhere nicer. He then took me out of town to show me this beautiful house, which had been built along with what was called the Mid-Ocean Golf Course and was owned by a white multi-millionaire called Broc Park, whose wife was the Ladies' champion golfer on the island. It was a truly magnificent place, both his house and the golf course.

He then took me back into town and pointed out a place called The Old Colony Club, which was for white people only. After I had played a couple of exhibitions I got a phone call from Broc Park asking if I did any coaching and although I hadn't done any before, I said yes, so he told me to "Phone for a taxi and tell the driver to bring you to the house by the side of the 14th tee on the Mid Ocean Golf Course," which I did. Broc Park, who would have been about 65 years old and a very smart man, paid the taxi driver and then took me through to his snooker room and asked me what I thought of his snooker table. I said it was the same type of table that we played on in England except for the cloth, which was an American pool cloth that is a much slower and cheaper cloth than English cloth. He then said, "Well, let's get on with it, I'll pay you £10 an hour so let's get started." He was not a very good player so I spent quite a bit of time showing him the basics of the game. We had been playing for about two hours when he said, "Right, let's stop for a while and go and have a cup of tea." As we sat down his servant brought the tea through before he looked at his watch and said that was about three hours. He then gave me £30 and paid the taxi driver to take me back to my hotel. I could not believe what was happening, money was obviously of no concern to him and yet again I was amazed at the lifestyles to which I was being included.

The morning after, Will Minors came to see me and gave me the rest of my itinerary and I found that I was only playing four matches in the first week. They took me out to show me the whole of the island. Most of the visitors used to hire a small motorbike to get around the island where everything was so laid back. I just could not believe how relaxed it was. Strangely, the police force that worked on the island were all from England, a couple of whom I knew.

I got a phone call to see if I wanted a game of golf on the Mid Ocean Golf Course and Broc said that I could use his friend's set of clubs, so he came and picked me up. What a game of golf it was, I have never seen such a beautiful course. After we finished he suggested going to The Old Colony Club for lunch, which we did. It was just like your typical upper-class English Club and it was not too long before they asked me if I had any free nights available to play there, to which I said yes. However, I told them they would have to book me through Will Minors as he had paid all the expenses for my trip and he would want to be there. They said they were very sorry to hear that as they did not allow coloureds in The Old Colony Club so that was the end of that, or so I thought.

The next morning I got up and went down for breakfast. I picked up a copy of the local paper and could not believe what I saw. The headline was:

JOHN SPENCER REFUSES TO PLAY AT THE OLD COLONY CLUB BECAUSE HIS COLOURED FRIENDS WERE NOT ALLOWED IN

After the headlines in the paper, I got a standing ovation as soon as I entered any club.

On the day Margot was due to fly in for the start of our honeymoon we were all waiting at the airport to meet her and I was very surprised to see Broc Park there. When she came through Customs she had a trolley with her suitcase on and was also carrying a parcel, which was quite big. This turned out to be a snooker cloth; apparently, Broc Park had got to know that Margot was coming over on the Monday and had phoned up Rileys Snooker in England and asked them to deliver a top quality cloth to Margot at home in Radcliffe so that she could bring it over with her. I now knew why Broc had come out to the airport to meet her.

OUT OF THE BLUE INTO THE BLACK

We had a wonderful honeymoon over there. I remember one time, Margot and I were sat on the steps of the hotel and two ladies were talking about a Portuguese Man of War, which had been washed up on the beach. We immediately said that we would have to go and have a look at this when one of the ladies said that it must have been about three inches in length. Margot and I just could not stop laughing as we thought it was a boat that had been washed up and not a sea creature!

I was a little sorry when my final exhibition came along but before I could start the match everybody in the club stood up shouting and cheering. The reason for this was that Broc Park had come into a 'coloured club' for the first time in his life and although it was a full house, they soon made plenty of room for him on the front row. On this particular night Margot was at a party at Broc Park's house, which was full of bankers, Senators and film stars from America. Despite this, she said that it was the most boring night of her trip and Broc Park had left this gathering to come and watch the snooker.

We had also met another wealthy man called Charlie, who owned a large chain of shops. When we were leaving he had insisted that we call at his house on the way to the airport. He took us round the back of the house where he had a swimming pool in the shape of a brandy bottle. In no time at all he showed us why the pool was this shape when he brought out brandy glasses and a couple of brandy bottles and filled three of them up. It was not long before we said we would have to go to catch the plane and he said, "Don't worry about the plane, I will get you there on time. It won't leave without you, I promise." By this time Margot and I had both had plenty of brandy. We did catch the plane, though only as we delayed take-off by twenty minutes, and when Margot and I got on with the hiccups all the passengers were giving us dirty looks for delaying them though I am glad to say that we were past worrying.

While we were in Bermuda we also met a couple called Chinky and Margaret Mellor, who we got very friendly with, and they later came over to England for a holiday. We arranged to pick them up at the airport and take them to their hotel, which was in the Lake District, so off we went in my car and got onto the M6. When Margot looked round to talk to them, she found that they were huddled together and their faces were as white as snow. Then I remembered that they were only used to going at 20 miles per hour in Bermuda and I was going at 60-plus, so I pulled into the next service station and said how sorry I was for not remembering the speed they had become used to in Bermuda.

A couple of weeks after we returned home I was playing an exhibition in Bristol and was in the middle of a frame when they called me to the phone. It was Broc Park and I told him that I was mid-game, so he told me to phone the operator and ask for "Bermuda 5" when an interval came, which I did. Within a couple of minutes I was speaking to Broc Park, who just wanted to thank me for all the pleasure that I had given him on my trip to Bermuda and for Margot taking the snooker cloth over for him. I still do not know how he found out which club I was playing at that night because Margot did not even know where I was playing.

OUT OF THE BLUE INTO THE BLACK

When Margot and I first married we lived with my mother while we looked for a house of our own. From the start it was pretty obvious that my mother and Margot did not get on too well together, mainly I think because my mother thought that she was so much younger than me and also due to the very short mini-skirts that Margot used to wear, even though they were all the rage at that time. I suppose my mother was a bit of a prude when it came to such things as regards Margot's outfits, and of course it would mean that she would be on her own for the first time were I to set up home elsewhere.

Our first house together was a bungalow in Sunningdale Avenue in Radcliffe. It was all ready to move into but I was worried about leaving my mother on her own for the first time, though Margot quite rightly said that as the house was ready she was moving in anyway and packed her bags. She said I could make up my mind whether I was going or not and after a couple of days I was missing her so much - and was now married to her - that I decided it was time to move in with her. Although it was not actually the first time I had left my mother on her own, as I had previously left her while in the RAF, it was harder for me to leave this time as unlike before, this time I would be leaving the house for good.

The first thing that I decided to do when I got to Sunningdale Avenue was to have a go at decorating the bathroom, which was only the second time in my life that I had tried anything like that. My first attempt in the prefab had turned out to be a disaster. This time, when I'd finished I was very pleased with myself and when Margot came home later I could not wait to show her the bathroom. The first thing that she said was, "Well it is very nice, but why are the flowers growing downwards?" I had only put the paper on upside down!

After about 18 months we started looking at another larger bungalow on the main Bury and Bolton Road and we had mentioned this to Margot's mother and father. It was not long after that Eric, Margot's father, came round and said that he could do us a deal with the bungalow on the Bury and Bolton Road as he had found out that the owner had a bridging loan and would let us have it for £24,000. On top of that, he would buy our bungalow in Sunningdale Avenue at our asking price for his secretary to live in, so it was all done and dusted in a very short space of time. It was a three-bedroom bungalow with an en-suite bedroom above the kitchen, which you got to by pulling a set of stairs down from the ceiling in the corridor. The kitchen had fitted units all the way round and also had an Aga cooker, which we did not know at the time was going to cause Margot a great deal of aggravation in the future. The lounge was the full length of the bungalow and had a fire built in the middle of the room. We virtually made the front half of the room the lounge and the other half was the bar area, which we could use when we had guests round. Otherwise we hardly ever used that half of the lounge.

Over the trees at the back was a huge farmer's field and at the front, opposite the back door of the house, was quite a big front garden with a beautiful lawn. There was a large brick double garage and of course, as is often the case, the car was always left on the driveway and instead we turned the garage into a storage unit, at the back of which was a tank in which oil went for the Aga cooker and the central heating. The bungalow was situated next door to the Jolly Carters pub and we soon got friendly with the landlord, who was called Stuart.

We had not been there very long when we went for a run-out in the car. We came across these two children who had a basket at the side of them with four puppies in it and a sign at the side reading 'Puppies given free'. So we went over to them and it turned out that their parents had told them that if they could not get rid of them then they would have to be put down. So Margot, without any thought, picked one and when we got back home she named it Kinky, which was after a Bluecoat at Morecambe Bay holiday camp.

We were sat in the lounge one night when Margot said that she could hear some strange noises coming from the back garden. When she went to the window and opened the curtains a big cow's face was looking at her which made her scream, so we had to go out into the back and drive them all back into the farmer's field. The following morning we then saw what a mess they had made of the garden so we immediately got on to a fencing company to come and put a 6ft fence along the bottom of the garden. A couple of days later Margot was having a bit of trouble with the Aga when my nephew Rodney, who was a mechanic, happened to come round and eventually got it working properly. The day after we had to go and see her mother and father about something and when we got back, everywhere in the kitchen was covered in soot as something had gone wrong with the Aga. The whole kitchen was black and it took us about two days before we managed to clean everything up, it was an absolute nightmare. After this, when I went away to play some snooker exhibitions and arrived back home, I noticed that there were dents appearing in the metal top of the Aga, which turned out to be where Margot had smashed it with a frying pan. It was always in the winter that Margot started having trouble with that Aga and at times it nearly drove her insane.

It was also at this time that we started going to a nightclub called Bennies, which was only about a mile from home and quite a few celebrities used to go there. It was quite a big place with a disco, restaurant and Robson's piano bar, which was named after the Manchester United footballer Bryan Robson who used to go in quite a lot. Other footballers that used to go in were Terry McDermott and Peter Reid and Noel Edmonds appeared once when we were there. We used to have a real good laugh as we never went in until after 11 o'clock and everyone had already had a few drinks, including us.

There was also another businessman called Ken Leary who used to join us in Bennies and he also owned a nightclub, called Phillips Park. One night he asked me if I would open a fish and chip shop for him that he was opening in Manchester, so a few days later Margot and I turned up at this fish and chip shop, which was upstairs. When we got upstairs there was not a soul in, and after about half an hour I was leaning out of the window with a fish in my hand shouting, "Come and get your fish here," but no one came although I believe that it did quite well eventually.

OUT OF THE BLUE INTO THE BLACK

One time we had a knock on the door and Margot answered it. It was a policeman who lived further down Bury and Bolton Road and said that our dog Kinky had "raped his bitch", which made Margot laugh. He then threatened Margot by saying that he knew her car number, which really annoyed her. She said, "Do not threaten me as I will go to the police." In the end she offered to pay for his dog to go to the vets but nothing came of it.

After our honeymoon, Margot had got herself a job as a receptionist at Pontin's Blackpool camp for the season. I did not have to drive home every day as I shared a chalet with Margot at Blackpool and had my own chalet at the Morecambe Bay and Southport camp, so I virtually had a holiday for the whole of the summer and all I had to do was to play a few frames of snooker and to judge a few of the competitions that they held, such as Miss Pontin's and Elegant Grandmother. Believe it or not, quite a lot of Grandmothers actually entered and won the Miss Pontin's competition as well. The winners of these camp competitions went on to the grand finals, which were held at the Albert Hall in London in October.

They also had cabaret on every night so it was like getting paid for having a holiday. It was during this time that a pal of mine from Walton-on-Thames was able to get Savile Row suits, which had gone out of fashion, for virtually nothing. He brought me a pile of them to see if I could sell them on the camps, which at the price was no problem as the three-piece suits were only costing me £15 and without trying I was getting £25. So at the holiday camps my chalet was more like a clothes store, while at home I even had two policemen who arrived in their panda car and bought some. I often wondered what our neighbours thought when they saw the two policemen in a panda car carrying these suits out of the house. Incidentally, one year when the camp managers arrived for one of the Miss Pontin's Royal Albert Hall finals, they found that two of them had the same Savile Row suit on. I had to get out of the way when I saw them as I had told all the managers that the suits were one-offs! Nevertheless, they kept on buying them.

What a life I was having; playing golf at Southport on two of the best courses in the country, then going to have a three-course meal which was ready for me as soon as I arrived, then cabaret all night and, other than one hour of snooker, my time was my own. Was I glad that I had decided to go and see Bill Armistead in Blackpool!

It was also on the holiday camps that I started to drink rather heavily. Before I went to the holiday camps I used to drink about five pints of lager before I started to feel a bit tipsy, but before the end of the season I had moved on to drinking about eight pints of draught lager before it began to affect me. Sometimes when some of the governors came up from the head office in Bournemouth and they started buying the drinks, I would finish up drinking a lot more than I should have done and end up as drunk as a lord. I also used to end up drinking with the Bluecoats on the camp and whoever was doing the cabaret act on that particular site at the time.

It was about this time that Alex Higgins, who in Belfast was a young amateur snooker star, was going to come over to play some exhibition matches in the Lancashire area. It was my mate Vince Laverty, who worked for the *Bolton Evening News*, who had set up the first challenge match in Bolton. He went to meet Alex off the boat from Belfast and took him to Jim Worsley's, who was the Chairman of the Bolton Snooker League. Jim was going to let Alex stay with him as he had also arranged quite a few exhibitions around the Lancashire area between Alex and myself. I must say that every exhibition that we played was a sell-out and add that we had some very good matches. He then decided to move house and went to live over towards Accrington, so we only played one or two exhibitions a week after that.

During the winter months I was still doing exhibitions for the Spastics Society and was doing about 56,000 miles a year travelling up and down the country for them. After I had played for them for a few years I suddenly thought of an idea, which eventually gave me one of the happiest moments of my life. That was that instead of just going to a club and playing an exhibition, I would go to a club and give seven players 200 starts and if they beat me I would forfeit my fee. So everywhere I went I used to pinch the *Yellow Pages* of snooker clubs in the area where I was playing. Margot got about 500 postcards printed with all this information on and then had to sit down and write all the addresses from the *Yellow Pages* on to the cards. We had to borrow some money from the bank to pay for all this. We had virtually given up hope of anything happening from this as for five or six days we had not had a reply and were very dejected. We thought we had lost our money after all the work Margot had put into it. Then after ten days four of these cards came through the letterbox, the next day some more arrived, then quite a lot came, and the two of us were dancing round the house like lunatics. Without a doubt it was certainly the happiest moment of my snooker career, even more so than winning the World Championship

One of the reasons that I was so happy was that with all the professionals that had played before me, I was the first to think of this idea. Not only were there bookings for a bit more money, but instead of driving all over the country night after night I could now arrange a week's bookings in one area and virtually choose which area I wanted to be in on a certain week, so it cut my mileage and my driving down from about 56,000 miles to about 30,000 miles. The one and only thing that could have gone wrong was if I lost two or three a week I could be out of pocket. The only reason that I set the start at 200 was that it meant that I was giving the best player in the club the equivalent of 30 start, but also I would only be giving the 7th best player in the club 30 start and I knew that not many clubs had more than three good players. As it happened I only lost one of these matches, which was in Wales where they had put the Welsh national team out against me. It finished up that in the last frame I made a 96 break with one red remaining, so I had to refuse a certain 100 break, as I wanted one snooker to win the match.

It was during these exhibitions that I first met Jimmy White and Tony Meo. Every time I played an exhibition in the London area these were two of the players I would play. I think they were about 15 years old at the time and what a great potter Jimmy was at that age. I was sure he would be a professional in the not too distant future and when he finally became a professional his game never changed. He certainly became the people's player and still is, and that is why wherever he plays it is always a full house. The only other one that could claim to do this was Alex Higgins, but for totally different reasons.

The BBC director in charge of the snooker at Sheffield once decided to give Alex Higgins a try in the commentary box. The match was between Ray Reardon and Eddie Charlton. He hadn't been in the box that long when Ray decided to leave the arena and go to the loo. Alex picked up the microphone and said, "There goes Dracula running out of blood, he's going for another pint." Needless to say, that was the end of his career as a commentator!

Another time I was commentating with Ted Lowe on one of Alex Higgins' matches and the night before Alex had been all round the Crucible watering all the plants. In the match Alex played a shot which smashed into the reds and sent the balls flying all over the table and Ted came in on the commentary, saying that Alex must have seen a plant there as he had a right slash at that one. Then the following day Ted and myself were commentating on Bill Werbeniuk's match with Dennis Taylor. Bill had just got down to play his shot when the crowd all started laughing and Ted went through to the director to ask what had happened. Apparently, when he had stretched over the table he broke wind. Eventually, when the laughing finally stopped, he got round to playing his shot and so I said on the commentary, "If he is going for this shot he has to go all out for it as it is no good being half-farted about it."

Chapter 7

On Top of the World, Ma!

Triple World Champion 1969, 1971 & 1977

I ENTERED the World Professional Snooker Championship for the first time in 1969 and had to play the toughest of the older professionals in the first round, which was John Pulman at the Wryton Stadium in Bolton. It was a sell-out for the whole week and in the final session I only needed one frame to win the match. But when Pulman was introduced for that session, the manner in which he entered suggested that it was he who only wanted one frame and that was why he was such a good professional. He never knew when he was beaten so I was more than delighted when I won the first frame. I mentioned this to John after the match and he said he would give me a tip and that was never to bother looking at the frame score as each frame you play starts off level and that is what you concentrate on. It was a tip that I am sure over the years has won me some matches that I would have lost without his advice, as there is so much of the game played in the mind.

I then took on Rex Williams in the semi-final, which I won by 37-12 and went on to play Gary Owen in the final at the Victoria Hall in London. I beat him 46-27 with a session to spare so the sponsor, Players No 6, put up a prize of 5000 Players No 6 coupons to the winner. I again managed to win and I was very surprised at the amount of things that you could get with those coupons. I also got a cheque for £1,050 for winning the World Championship.

After that I had to go on to the Ideal Homes Exhibition in London where I had been booked by Rileys Snooker to play exhibitions and trick shots for the rest of the week. It was fascinating as the next stall to us was the BBC Radio 1 stall and throughout the week in my exhibitions I made 13 centuries to the song *Lily the Pink*, which was also one of my favourite songs at that time. It also surprised me how many film stars and celebrities were there; everywhere you looked there seemed to be a recognisable face. One day, one of the girls from one of the exhibition stalls invited me out to lunch. She told me to get dressed up as we were going somewhere special and I thought my luck was in - and of course said yes. When she came for me, we set off and I thought we would be going somewhere out of the exhibition centre. However, she took me to the British Gas stall where a table was set for two and we had to sit there in front of a whole audience of people passing by and eat our lunch. It was very nice but I felt like I was in a shop window, which I suppose I was; she thought it was a great laugh at my expense.

The 1971 World Championship was played in November 1970 in Australia and my first match was against eight-times World Champion John Pulman at Wagga Wagga, which I won by 23 frames to 14. John, being the true professional that he was, never gave up trying right up to the last frame. After the first session had ended we went to the car and he jumped into the driver's seat. At the first road junction he nearly turned the car over by hitting what they called a silent policeman, which was a circular piece of concrete about four inches high and two foot in diameter. They were placed in the middle of the road at all the crossroads, to stop you cutting corners. It scared him so much that he got out of the driver's seat and gave me the car keys whereupon I became the designated driver for the next two days.

I managed to beat Pulman quite comfortably and was then drawn to play Ray Reardon in the semi-final at Parramatta Working Men's Club who, unknown to us, had been to the press and given them a story declaring that the conditions and organisation of the tournament were not particularly good. In fact, when I got to Parramatta to play Reardon, before the match had started John Pulman got up and made a speech and told everyone there that what had appeared in the newspaper that day was nothing to do with either himself or me and we thought that the organisation for the tournament had been good. This brought a great round of applause from the crowd and no doubt put them on my side during my semi-final match. They were applauding nearly every shot that I played against Reardon and I won by 34-15.

The final was against Warren Simpson at the Chevron Hilton Hotel and what a character he was; he would do anything for a laugh. We were booked into the Chevron Hilton and the rule was that everything would be paid for up to 10pm at night and then any drinks you had after that would be charged to your account. Not surprisingly, Pulman's bill was by far the biggest.

OUT OF THE BLUE INTO THE BLACK

It was in this match that I would say I probably played the best shot that I have ever played. The red was about 18 inches from the left hand black pocket, the white was on the baulk line about 6 inches from the right hand cushion and I thought, if I can screw it back a couple of feet I will have a chance of the blue. Well, I played the shot and must have hit it better than I have ever hit it before as the white screwed back in and out of baulk to finish nicely on the blue. Warren could not believe it and he stopped the game for about five minutes, walking along the rows of spectators saying things like, "Have you ever seen anything like that? It is not possible, he is not human." This went on for about five minutes before I could take my next shot and at the end of the session Warren was still talking about that shot. I must admit that throughout my career I have never played another shot like it. I also created another record against Warren and that was to make three centuries in four frames. I went on to win the final comfortably, the score being 42-31, even though I lost one session very easily after having a late night out. I must confess it taught me a lesson and I never did it again throughout my career.

One of my best-ever winning streaks came when I was playing Norman Squire, the Australian professional, during the World Championship. Norman led six frames to three but I closed out the session with three winning frames. I won all six frames in session three and the first six frames in session four. Norman then put an end to my winning run of fifteen frames but by that point, I was home and dry. Mark Williams, in his interview after his victory over Quentin Hann in the 2004 World Championships, said his successive thirteen winning frames was probably some kind of record - he obviously knew little about my 15 consecutive frames all those years ago.

Norman Squire was also a big gambler. He took me to the dog track one night and I could not believe what I was seeing. They had ten greyhounds in a race and at the first bend it was carnage as many of the dogs were just knocked out of the race, so I did not have a bet all evening which was the first time I had ever done that at the dogs.

In 1977 I was the first player to win the World Championship at the Crucible Theatre in Sheffield. This was sponsored by Embassy and had come a long way from the 1969 days. In the final, I played Cliff Thorburn for a prize of £6,000. The Crucible is a wonderful venue. I used to get goosebumps as I drove along the M62 and down the M1 into Sheffield. I would say that the Crucible did more for snooker than any player did. There had been talk about changing the venue to somewhere which would hold more spectators as the Crucible only holds about 950 people, but the atmosphere there was tremendous.

At times you feel that the crowd are on top of you, especially when your form is a bit wanting. The Benson & Hedges, which was played at the Wembley Conference Centre, could double the crowds the Crucible had and could also boast a pretty good atmosphere itself. But for the tension alone, the Crucible is the only place to have the World Championship. It is something that you cannot explain until you have played there. The butterflies in my stomach and the sense of anticipation I felt just approaching the place the night before I was due to play is something that money cannot buy.

OUT OF THE BLUE INTO THE BLACK

I remember that, in the first morning session against Cliff, I lost the first three frames and the following morning I again lost the first three. On the third day Del Simmons, who was my manager, decided that he would get me up early and take me for a walk round Sheffield centre where we happened to see two car drivers out of their cars at the traffic lights having a fight. It seemed rather comical at that time of day although we did not know what had happened to cause this. We eventually got back to the hotel and this time I won the first three frames of the session. However, I then went on to lose the next three frames so that was the last of my early morning walks around Sheffield - though had there been a road rage incident each time I went out, I may well have continued my first session improvement!

Chapter 8

Pot Black

The Snooker Revolution 1969-1980

IT WAS the *Pot Black* series, an idea that Ted Lowe had brought to television, which finally produced widespread recognition for snooker. It was a one-frame knockout tournament for eight players and you had to try and get it over in twenty minutes, which obviously did not happen that many times so they had to edit it to fit in with the BBC TV slot.

The first *Pot Black* was played at the old Gosta Green studio in Birmingham immediately after Christmas 1969, when Ray Reardon beat me in the final. I got my revenge the following year, beating him at the same stage. As this was a one-frame knockout tournament, we all agreed that the total prize money should be shared between the eight players, which in the first one was about £250 each.

The viewing figures for this tournament meant that *Pot Black* had really put snooker on the map. Of course, the first series was in black and white but apparently it still claimed almost 5 million viewers each week. I would say that half of these were women who certainly got interested in the game, even more so when it was televised in colour. I think that a big part of this was the players wearing dress suits and bow ties and also the fact that women at that time were still not allowed into most of the snooker rooms in their local clubs. Due to the successful viewing figures the BBC decided to lengthen the series to sixteen programmes and when colour television arrived in 1971 snooker on the box really took off. The venue for *Pot Black* was changed to the Pebble Mill studios and the number of celebrities that came to see it went through the roof. Memorably, it was here that Ted Lowe came out with his famous line on TV when he said in his commentary, "For those watching in black and white, the yellow is next to the blue."

We all used to stay at the Strathallen Hotel in Birmingham for the four days after Christmas while filming *Pot Black*. I remember one year John Alderton came up and when we were all in the bar, playing tricks on one another, he shouted the waitress and asked her if she could get him an egg. He then took the egg off her and put it in his mouth, long side up, and asked if any of us could do that. Before any of us could move or reply, Alex Higgins was there and had taken the egg and put it in his mouth. John Alderton just turned to Alex and said, "Well done," and tapped him on the chin, breaking the egg while still in his mouth. I must say that Alex took it well and had a good laugh about it after and no doubt in the near future someone else would fall for the same old Laurel and Hardy trick as Alex did.

In 1974 Joe Davis himself came up and what a character he turned out to be. He had us all in stitches with some of the stories that he told us and, when I said something naughty to him, he just threw what was left of his drink over me and had a good laugh about it. That is when I realised he was one of the boys and not the snob that I had imagined he would be after what I had heard about him from different people. He was obviously a completely different person when he was at the snooker table.

I played in all the *Pot Blacks* from 1969 through to 1980, and then took part again in the 1984-1985 series. I was runner-up in the first *Pot Black* in 1969, and then I won it in 1970, 1974 and 1976, and finally was runner-up in 1984. Then they moved it to the Norbreck Castle Hotel in Blackpool where I was signed up by the BBC to spend my time with Ted Lowe in the commentary box for the next three years. The amazing thing about this programme was that when I was going round the country playing my exhibitions and happened to be on television playing in *Pot Black* at the same time, many people would ask me if it was live even though I was stood in front of them in a different part of the country! The interest in the series was huge and the whole conversation during the intervals at exhibitions was about *Pot Black*.

One of the funniest times I can remember when commentating on the first *Pot Black* series with Ted Lowe was when Fred Davis had a difficult shot to play. He had his right leg over the corner of the table trying to reach the white but decided that he could not reach it, so he got the cue rest out, then put it away, before he leaned over and played it left-handed. Ted had already begun his commentary by saying, "And that is the difference with Fred Davis. Now 67 years of age, he cannot get his leg over anymore." He suddenly realised what he had said and tried to get out of it by saying he "prefers to use his left hand", before the commentary stopped for five minutes and began again after we had managed to stop laughing.

We were also invited out to New Zealand to make a series of *Pot Black* and what a surprise for us all whilst over there. We were waiting in the hotel for the transport to the venue when round the corner came eight Rolls-Royces - one for each player. This just goes to show how highly the series was regarded and how much Ted Lowe's *Pot Black* had done for snooker, not only in Britain but also across the globe. In 1997 I was invited to take part in a Seniors Pot Black, sponsored by Henderson Investors, in a mini-revival of the tournament. However, this was right in the middle of my depression from Myasthenia Gravis, so we travelled to Goodwood by train as I was in no state to drive. Predictably and unsurprisingly, Dennis Taylor beat me in the first round.

Chapter 9

Green Baize Glory

Other Tournaments 1971-1981

IN 1972, the third Park Drive 2000 was played on the Sunday with the world championship final against Higgins starting on the Monday. It was at the Radcliffe Civic Hall and the two finalists were Alex Higgins and myself. It was a complete sell-out, played at the time of the national power cuts, so they had to get a generator in for the lighting which made it very difficult to play. It was a close game, which I managed to win 4-3 after losing the first two frames, and earned £750 for the win while Alex received £550. We went into the last frame all level but I felt I was on top and won the final frame 62-14. It was a match that did not live up to the big break snooker that everyone had expected and I am sure the lighting had a lot to do with that, though the tension and the safety play throughout the match made up for it.

The following week we were due to meet in the World Professional Championship Final at Selly Park British Legion Club, over the best of 73 frames. The power strike was still on so, again, a generator was brought in. I remember when we were going for the afternoon session on the fifth day, the lift at the hotel stopped for a couple of minutes and the traffic going to the venue was terrible as all the traffic lights were out. I had a slight bump in the car through trying to get there on time in difficult conditions, but eventually arrived at the venue, which was packed to capacity. You could not see anything, there were bodies everywhere, sat on beer crates or whatever they could find. The snooker that was played in those conditions was tremendous and the crowd were going crazy, shouting and cheering nearly every shot. There were plenty of breaks and some great snooker played but in the end Alex beat me fair and square with a late flourish by 37 frames to 32. But I was not too disappointed as I thought that I had played exceptionally good snooker considering the conditions, though I admit Alex played better. Unfortunately this was the year that the sponsors for the tournament had pulled out at the last minute and the total prize money was now £800, which was the £100 entry fees from the eight professionals that had entered. This was split up 60% to the winner and 40% to the runner-up, which meant that Alex got £480 and I got £320.

One of the funny things that happened between me and Alex around this time was when, at the end of an exhibition we had played down in London, Alex came to me to see if I was going home to Manchester and if so, could I give him a lift. I said, "Yes, no problem," so in he got and we set off for Manchester. It was not long before his feet were up near the windscreen and the cigarettes were coming out fast and furious. I eventually got him home to Cheadle where I happened to mention the mess he had made in the car and told him I would not be giving him a lift anywhere else. The next time we were down South he again came to ask me if I would give him a lift home and I just said no. His reply was simply "OK" and off he went. That went on every time I was playing him but he never ever got upset about it.

The 1973 Norwich Union Tournament, which was played in London, was probably the most satisfying tournament I ever played in. It was the first tournament I had played since the car accident I had in North Wales when my cue was broken into four pieces. Cliff Curtis from Rileys managed to stick it back together and this was the tournament I was going to use it in for the first time. I went on to beat John Pulman by 8 frames to 7 and I don't think that record will ever be broken, winning a tournament with a four-piece cue! I also won this tournament again in 1974 by beating Ray Reardon by 10 frames to 9, this time with a two-piece cue as my old cue had started to come apart again. In fact I was the only winner of this event as they withdrew their sponsorship after the 1974 tournament.

In 1975 I was the first winner of The Benson & Hedges Tournament, played at Fulham's West Centre Hotel. I played Reardon in the final and it was made more exciting by the fact that it went to a black ball finish. It was one of the best tournaments on the circuit and well attended as only the top sixteen players were invited. Jim Elkins, who became the tournament director after Len Owen, bore a remarkable likeness to myself and was constantly being asked for his autograph by fans thinking it was me. He did not mind this and sometimes actually signed them. It was at this tournament that I met Joe Coral the bookmaker, who asked me why I had never opened an account with his company as I had always had my credit account with Ladbrokes. When I said that I would love to have a credit account with them, he got all my details and opened an account for me there and then, as he was also mad about playing snooker as well as watching it.

When Del Simmons got involved in the game in 1975/76, he had 16 players signed on his books, including Alex Higgins and myself, going under the banner of the International Snooker Agency (ISA). He bought premises in Bristol, which were eventually to become the WPBSA headquarters. Del was also in business with Sean Connery and Bobby Moore at the time. Eventually a new board was founded, but unfortunately it was made up mostly of players and players' managers so there was not much done to promote the game, especially if it did not suit their own interests.

In 1976 I was the first winner of the Irish Benson & Hedges Tournament, which was held at the Green Isle Hotel, Dublin. The trophy I received for winning it is the only trophy that I still possess, as it was a Waterford Crystal cut-glass trophy, unlike the metal cups that we used to get in those days. I flew to Dublin to take part and was met as usual by Kevin Norton, the tournament organiser. When we got back to Dublin we met the governor of Benson & Hedges who asked me if I would like to have a tour of the factory and see how the cigarettes were made. As we were walking down a passage between all the stacks of cigarettes, a bright yellow door caught my eye as it was up near the ceiling and did not seem to have any steps leading to it. I asked him what the door was for and he had to admit that he did not know, but he said he would find out and let me know later on that day. When I saw him hours later, he said that all the electricity supply for the building was in that room but you could only get in if you had a ladder that was long enough. It must have made sense to somebody, I suppose.

Once again, Bensons and the organiser Kevin Norton put on a really good tournament, to which most of the invited players would take their wives or partners. The Irish B & H was a special competition for me as I count myself a good friend of Norton who would be on the go all day and every day to make sure that things ran like clockwork. If he wanted any interviews for TV he knew that he could always count on me to do them.

Though I was happy to visit Southern Ireland, the Troubles in Northern Ireland meant I and many other sportsmen and celebrities reckoned it was just too unstable to visit at that time. I remember in 1977 when I was World Champion and playing exhibitions nearly every night, out of the blue I got a phone call from a gentleman in Northern Ireland asking me if I would go over and play an exhibition at his snooker club. I told him that I would not be going across the water at that particular time but he kept phoning me and each time he was offering me more money. He finished up offering me £500 for the one night. Tempted, had he left it at that, I might have gone, but then he went on to say, "You'll be safe at my club, as it is situated between the police station and the army barracks." That was enough to ensure I didn't go!

OUT OF THE BLUE INTO THE BLACK

Then, would you believe, a few months later I got an invitation from Frank Carson inviting me to play in his charity golf day at Clandeboye Golf club which was just outside Belfast. Of course, there was no way I could get out of playing in a charity golf day so I finished up going to Belfast for no money. We stayed at the Europa Hotel and I remember going to the toilet and the graffiti on the wall said, "BUY NOW WHILE THE SHOPS LAST!" There were also soldiers on guard all round the hotel, which gives you an indication of how serious things were back then.

After the golf had finished we went upstairs in the hotel where the cabaret was taking place and I was sat at a table with a reporter from the *Belfast Telegraph*. The news came through that Bobby Sands had gone into a coma, and I thought to myself, 'What a night to come to Belfast for the first time,' and I promise you that there wasn't a spare seat on the first flight at 6.30am out of Belfast the next morning.

I have only been back to Northern Ireland once since then and that was in the early Nineties when I received a request to go and visit a gentleman who was in a nursing home on the outskirts of Belfast. It was his 100th birthday on the day of my visit and he was snooker mad and apparently a great fan of mine. So I travelled over on his 100th birthday and spent about two hours with him talking about snooker while he was still drank his whisky.

In 1978 I was also invited to take part in the *Jim'll Fix It* TV programme with this young lad who had written to Jimmy Saville asking to play a game of snooker with me. I remember the band that was on that same show as being Hot Chocolate, one of my favourite bands at that time. And who did the 12-year-old boy turn out to be? None other than that cheeky Scouser John Parrott! So I suppose I would be the first professional player he would have played against. Another memorable moment happened in 1978, following my first round exit to Perrie Mans in the World Championship. However, it didn't turn out to be so bad for me as Nick Hunter, who was the executive producer for Snooker, Rugby League, Bowls and Cricket, asked me if I would give commentating a try, which I did and I finished up doing that and thoroughly enjoying it for 19 years. So that defeat turned out to be pretty good for me. And I did have some fun commentating...

In January 1979 (and getting back to what I was really good at - playing), at the Holsten Pils Lager Tournament in Slough, I could have had another record. Against Cliff Thorburn, in a match decided by the aggregate score over six frames, I made a 147 in the second. When I was on the final black I got down to play it but let the cue go over the top of the white and fell on the table for a laugh. David Taylor, 'The Silver Fox' himself, came running out of the audience thinking that I had fainted. Luckily, after he had gone back to his seat I got down again and potted the black. Had I missed it I would have made a right fool of myself but that is how I have been all my life, anything for a laugh. Unfortunately for me the camera crew had gone off for a tea break and missed it. Still, the sponsors gave me £50 extra for making it and that is why when the BBC covered any tournament after that, they filmed every frame that was played in case someone should make a 147 break.

OUT OF THE BLUE INTO THE BLACK

It was in 1979 that Margot and I went off to India where I was going to play in the Garware Paints Invitation tournament at the Bombay Gymkhana, which was a six-man round-robin tournament. Every match that was played during this week was in front of a full house and I went on to win it by winning four of my five matches. The first prize for this was £2,000 and I also won a further £200 for the highest break, which was 108, and a trophy for the 'Man of the Series' award. It was quite funny that with all the countries I had been to on my travels, the only place that Margot wanted to come with me was to India. She absolutely loved it when we got over there; in fact she came with me three times and enjoyed every minute that she was there. She made quite a lot of friends on these trips and they went out of their way to make Margot happy. It was after one of these trips to India that when we got home half of the front lawn at Bury and Bolton Road had disappeared and a lovely driveway had appeared, going round the front of the house, which meant that we did not have to keep reversing out on to the main road. Unbeknown to me, Margot had arranged this with David before we left and I must say he made a fabulous job of it.

When I was flying to Australia before the Winfield Australian Masters tournament in 1980, the plane landed at Singapore and the steward came out and said that we would have to stay on the plane while they sorted something out. They then went to a man seated about ten rows in front of me and they must have been talking to him for a couple of hours. Then, as they left the plane, another two got on and went talking to the same man. This occurred at the time when a lot of hijackings were taking place and understandably made us nervous, as we were on the ground for seven hours before they escorted this man off the plane. It was a relief to get in the air again with the next stop being Perth in Australia. The thing that really annoyed me when you landed in Australia was that you had to stay in your seats while the stewards walked through the plane with sprays, which came down all over you, and you had to sit there and take it. I found out later that the spray was to try and prevent anybody bringing any infectious diseases into the country. I never did find out what the guy in Singapore had done or was planning on doing, but maybe that's for the best.

The Winfield Australian Masters was a tournament organised by Eddie Charlton in 1980 but it was a different format to the normal tournament, as each round was the aggregate score over three frames. I went on and won this tournament, beating Dennis Taylor in the final. We went and played it again in 1981 but this time I lost to Tony Meo in the final. It was on this trip that I came down for breakfast and Perrie Mans and Rex Williams were sat at a table having breakfast. They seemed to be arguing so I went over and joined them and asked them what they were arguing about. Rex said that Perrie kept pigeons and if any cats came near them he would kill the cat, so in the end Perrie said to Rex, "What would you do if you had a race horse and a tiger went after it?" Rex replied immediately, "I would find out how fast it could fucking run," and with that we sat there laughing our heads off.

OUT OF THE BLUE INTO THE BLACK

I was flying back from Australia one time and was sitting next to Dennis Taylor on the back row of the club class seats, with just a curtain behind us. About half an hour after we had taken off this massive boot came under the curtain between our feet and without thinking Dennis called the stewardess over. He said, "Excuse me, but could you tell me if this is a club foot?" Before we could say anything the stewardess had gone for the chief steward, who came to see what the problem was. When he realised, it finished up with all three of us in stitches.

In 1981 there was a World Team Championship which was staged at the Hexagon Theatre in Reading. The British team included David Taylor, Steve Davis and myself and we took things very seriously. We had a good practice together and decided that when one of us was playing, the other two had to sit on two seats we had reserved in the balcony. The thinking was that whoever was playing could just look up and the other two could take the pressure off by making him laugh or something. Whatever it was, it certainly worked as we went on to win the tournament.

We were staying at the Ramada hotel for this tournament and myself, Steve and Robbo, his driver, must have had too much to drink and the three of us finished on the floor of the bar area after everyone had gone to bed. We just could not stop laughing and it must have been half an hour before we managed to get to our feet. To this day I still do not know what we were laughing at, although I know that drink had more than a lot to do with it.

The most money I won in a tournament was on reaching the fourth round of the British Open at Derby in 1987, when I played Jimmy White and was beating him up to the last couple of frames. One frame I will always remember was when I needed five snookers and managed to get them. After the game Barry Hearn, then Jimmy's manager, said that I shouldn't be getting that close to beating Jimmy and had given him a fright. I got more money for this match than I had received for winning the World Championship, which was £6,000 in 1977. I received £9,000 for the match against Jimmy, which was only the quarter-final.

Chapter 10

A Life Less Ordinary

A Shark Tale

I STARTED playing golf nearly every day during the early Sixties and got down to a handicap of 10 and was soon playing in all the golf pro-am and celebrity tournaments. In those days that was what all the professional golfers had to play in to make their money. Golf virtually took over my life when I was not competing in tournaments or exhibitions and was playing or practicing seven days a week, weather permitting. In the celebrity tournaments, about six of the competitors would perform their acts on stage in the evening after an enjoyable day of golf, so to me it was a great life I was leading.

I even went to Portugal for one pro-am before BBC2 invited me to play in the Pro-Celebrity golf tournament at the famous Gleneagles Hotel Golf Course in Scotland, where I played with Lee Trevino. What a character he was - he had us laughing all day long and on this particular morning Ronnie Corbett had been working in Newcastle and was flying up by helicopter to play. We were all stood at the front door of the hotel when this helicopter came down and landed on the lawn outside the front door of the hotel. Out stepped Ronnie Corbett and Trevino asked us, "Who is that guy there?" We told him his name was Ronnie Corbett and that he was his partner for the morning. Trevino replied, "My partner? I make bigger fucking divots!"

When I played alongside him in the afternoon, he just never stopped and had us in stitches all the time. I remember on the third hole I hit the best drive I had ever hit in my life. For the next one I asked Lee what iron he would use and out came his book with all the yardages on. After about a minute he turned to me and told me to use a 7 iron. I did this, hitting the ball as good as ever, except this time the ball fell about 30 yards short of the green. Trevino then came over and asked me what I had used and when I said a 7 iron, he said that I needed a 5 iron, but for him it would have been a 7 iron. He then walked away laughing. That was how he was all the way round the course and you can imagine what he was like in the bar at night telling us all his golf stories. It was one of the funniest days of my life.

I then got an invitation from a chap called Robert Winsor to play in one of his celebrity pro-am golf tournaments, which was being held in North London. On this particular day I set off to drive down South and called in at a hotel in Birmingham just off the M6, where I used to have a game of kalooki (cards) whenever I was in that area. It turned out to be my lucky day as I won £800. The guys I was playing with asked if I wanted a game of backgammon, as a friend of theirs would be coming soon. I said no as I had to leave for a prior arrangement and needed to be there for a certain time. I thought that the person they were bringing in would be a professional gambler and a good player; backgammon is a far more professional game than most people think so I decided to make my apologies and leave. I then set off for London. Approaching my destination, I telephoned Robert to see which was the best hotel near the golf course. He said, "Forget the hotel, you can come and stay with us at our house in Totteridge," and then gave me the directions. When I got there I could not believe it, the bar was crowded with celebrities like Morecambe and Wise, motor racing's James Hunt, Des O'Connor, Richard Harris and many more stars from the TV world. He then got the maid to show me to my room and it was truly magnificent.

I had a shower, got changed and went downstairs to join them. After I had a couple of drinks I went over to Robert and Grace Kennedy, his wife, and asked them what charity the event was for. He said it was in aid of powered wheelchairs for disabled children. I asked him how much they cost and he said £241 each, so having just won £800 on the way down I told him I would buy one. He seemed taken aback and amazed by my offer so I took him out to the car where I had left the money and gave him the £241. He then came over to me later on in the night and said that it was the first time that had ever happened and that whenever I was playing in the London area I had to stay at his house. I was not to worry if they were not at home as the maids would look after me and with that he gave me a key to his million pound house, which had a window the full length of the lounge overlooking the massive garden at the back of the house. When I looked out all I could see was about 200 pink flamingos just strolling round and round the huge garden, which was one of the most relaxing sights I have ever seen. Buying that one wheelchair must have saved me about £2,000 in hotel bills around the London area!

What a day it was, especially seeing the kiddies' faces when they got their powered wheelchairs. It sent a shiver up my back knowing that I had bought one for them, seeing their faces light up and then, when they had got used to the chairs, riding around the golf club in them.

This was the first pro-am I had ever played in and I couldn't believe it when they told me I was partnering the American professional, Corey Pavin, who was also playing his first match in this country. After this event I became very friendly with Robert and Grace. One time when I was visiting them, Robert took me to the hospital where his pregnant wife Grace was due to have the baby. We had only been at the hospital for about an hour when he came to me and gave me the keys to his Rolls-Royce as Grace had gone into labour. He asked me to drive myself home. The drive back to his house should have taken half an hour, but it took me at least two hours, as it was the first time that I had been in a Rolls-Royce - what a fabulous time I had in that car, driving round London, posing! Well, how often do you get the chance?

I also played a lot for the Variety Club of Great Britain on their golf pro-am/celeb-am circuit and got to know quite a lot of golf professionals and stars. One pro-am I will always remember was the Benson & Hedges, which was played at York. I was in a team with a director of a company from Southampton, who was known on the circuit as the worst loser you could ever meet. Nick Faldo was our professional and we stood on the 16th tee with no chance of winning. Nick hit a long drive into the trees on the right and when we had all driven off we walked to where the balls had landed. Nick just walked into the trees and chopped his ball back onto the fairway. Eventually, when we got back to the clubhouse Nick had been reported for playing out of turn on the 16th hole. I had to go in front of the committee to let them know what had happened so they took no action against Nick. In fact, as far as I was concerned he was quite funny and made me laugh all the way round the course with some of his antics and the tales he told. Also, if you were in doubt about your next shot he would be there to help you.

I had a good friend called Paul Gaskell who hailed from Bolton but had moved to the Isle of Man. He got together with sports people and television stars to promote the pro and celeb-ams at golf on behalf of the charity SPARKS. I was one of the first to agree to support his tournaments - in fact, I used to get an invitation to them all.

One tournament that Paul put on was a celeb-am at Wentworth in Surrey. Everything was more expensive there, and while we paid £2 for a caddie wherever else we played, at Wentworth it cost you £5, though of course they were professional caddies and within three holes they just gave you the club that you needed for the next shot. You did not have to worry if you hit the ball as you usually did, as it would still travel the right distance for you. The celeb that was playing in my four-ball, and was well known for being a bit of a cheat, had hit his ball in the rough. Apparently he had found the ball and kept kicking it with his foot nearer to the green, but did not say anything to anyone. Eventually he declared that he had found it and said to the caddy, "What do you think it is from here, a 7 iron?" and the professional caddie said, "Not yet sir."

Another time I was playing in the Surrey Police pro-am golf day and the pro I was with was John Cook, who was one of the bright stars of that time. I was on the putting green when Ken Barrington, the cricketer, who I knew quite well, came over and said, "A tip for you John. When you are putting on this course, everything falls to the road." He then set up a putt for me on the putting green and sure enough it looked like a slight left to right break, but actually went slightly right to left. As soon as we got on the first tee I told John Cook, who was our professional, about this and sure enough he had a straightish putt on the first green. After having a good look at it he came over to me and said, "Be it on your head. I'm going to give it a couple of inches outside the hole," and sure enough he holed the putt. He came over and thanked me, which made me feel good. We had now reached the sixth hole and I had lost my ball in the trees so I was out of the hole. I was stood talking to some of the spectators when John Cook shouted to me to help him with the line of his putt. It made me feel great in front of all the spectators for them to see a professional asking me to go across the green to help him with the line of his putt! I went over to him and he said to me, "Where is the fucking road?" As the green was completely surrounded by trees and neither of us could make out where the road was, I was nearly on the floor laughing about this.

OUT OF THE BLUE INTO THE BLACK

I was always going down to Wentworth playing in company and celebrity golf days, arranged for me by Del Simmons. I got very friendly with two of his friends, Bill Bigmore and John Davies, who turned out to be insurance brokers under the name of Bigmore Tubbs. It was not long before we had all our insurance with them for the clubs.

A couple of years later, John Davies phoned me up to see if I was interested in going to Orlando in Florida. He had found a deal to stay at a place called Coca Beach, which was just down the road from Orlando, for just £81 each. There was a golf course just round the corner, so off we went to Cocoa Beach for a week's holiday. On the first day we were going to have a game of golf when we noticed this crowd of people on a small hill on the other side of the road. We wandered across to see what was happening and this fellow said that a rocket was due to be fired off from Cape Canaveral. Within five minutes we could see this rocket high in the sky; it had virtually zoomed over our heads in seconds and after it had gone this fellow told us to put our hands over our ears. Sure enough, there was a deafening noise and the ground seemed to shake under our feet after the rocket was long out of sight.

We then decided to go to the golf course for a round of golf and after about three holes one of our balls had gone towards the water. As we were looking for it we saw an alligator on the edge of the water, so from then on any ball that went towards the water was deemed to be a lost ball - for safety reasons! The next day we decided to have a visit to Disney World and I must say it was better than we could ever have imagined. It was so colourful and at every turning there was something going on. You could just walk into a booth, sit down in a chair and look through a monitor and you would be dive-bombing over London, France or anywhere else you would like to see. There were shows going continuously with groups passing in every national costume you could think of, endless parades marching by and bands producing all kinds of ebullient music. There was also a beautiful hotel right at the front, which was no doubt for the very wealthy people, and at the back of the hotel was a beautiful golf course. It was hard to believe that they could get so much life and colour into one area.

The best of all these charity golf days was at Northenden Golf Club near Manchester, where they used to have what they called an Irish night on the Friday before the golf day. When the teams of three were announced they auctioned the teams off and my pal Max Brown, who was one of the organisers of the event, had arranged that the third member of our team was Greg Norman, who had just arrived in this country. We had to bid quite a lot to keep our team before they then split up all the money into three prizes and the rest went to charity. The day after, we went down and played the round of golf. On the 17th tee we were leading by one and the 18th was a hole that was driveable. We stood on the tee and Greg pulled out an iron. Max and myself had a go at him as we wanted to see him drive the green and after a lot of persuading he got out his driver. However, he hooked it right into all the trees and finished with a 5, the same as Max and myself, so instead of winning it outright we had to share the first and second prize between six of us, meaning we got about £100 less than we would have got with a four at the last. I then got hold of Sam Torrance and told him what had happened and he said, "Leave it to me and don't say anything else to Greg about it." So Sam went round all the other pros and told them what had happened and the next thing was they all began to come upstairs and start winding Greg up for not taking an iron off the last tee. Angered, Greg dragged them all up to the bar where Max and I were stood and said, "Just tell them what you said to me when we were stood on the last tee." Without thinking, I said, "If you told me to take the pink instead of the black do you think I would listen?" With that he dived on me and had me on the floor before the others managed to pull him off. In the end he had to laugh himself.

At another tournament where I was partnering Greg we came to a par three and I asked him, "What should I take here, Greg, a three?" His immediate reply was, "I will be satisfied with a fucking 10 the way you are playing." Then on the next green I had hit two good shots and was down on my putt when a baby started crying. The mother was doing everything to try and calm the baby when Greg said, "Don't worry, the way he has been playing has made me want to cry."

I think that one of the funniest times I had was when I had been booked to do a show at the army barracks at the Curragh in Ireland on the Monday after the Irish Benson & Hedges, which had finished on the Sunday night when we all gone to bed at 3.00am, drunk as lords. My manager then was the late Del Simmons, a real character who unknown to me had talked Cliff Thorburn into coming along to the Curragh to play me in the exhibition. We had to be at the Curragh by 10am, as we had to catch our flight back to England at 2pm on the Monday. I remember walking into the army barracks as clearly as if it was yesterday. The lino was glistening and there was a lovely fire at the end of the room. We immediately made a beeline for the fire and sat round it, all three of us suffering stomach upsets caused by the drink from the evening before. I don't know who told him about this but soon after arriving the Sergeant Major appeared with three drinks for us and said they would settle our stomachs if we too drank it down in one. We did this and before we knew where we were another three appeared. Eventually we went through to the snooker room where I suppose there must have been about fifty soldiers waiting for us. They didn't have a referee so Del said he would do it, while in the meantime these drinks still kept appearing.

We eventually started the match and after a few minutes Cliff managed to pot a red. There was then a 'peep peep peep' sound from a calculator, which unknown to us Del had brought in, and then he shouted "One". The blue went in followed by more 'peeps' and Del saying "Six". There wasn't a murmur from the soldiers and the drinks were still coming, one after the other, which turned out to be brandy and port. We managed to get through the seven frames and some trick shots. Later we were talking to the soldiers, who said they thought the calculator idea was terrific but they had been told before we arrived that they had not to make a sound while we were playing. That was why they did not laugh at Del's antics even though they wanted to.

We left for the airport and I remember it was the day that seatbelts were made compulsory in Ireland. We were on our way through Dublin when Cliff suddenly wanted to go to the toilet. Del had seen a closed down garage and he said to the driver, "Pull in there so that Cliff can have a slash." Cliff got behind the car but as soon as he had started Del told the driver to drive off. This left Cliff stood in the middle of Dublin on an unused car forecourt, having a slash, not even realising the car had gone!

At the airport as we were checking-in later we noticed Lauren Bacall over the other side of the check-in desk. Cliff shouted over to her, "Hi Lauren - how's Humph (Humphrey Bogart - her husband)?" She just looked over at us and carried on through the check-in, she must have wondered who the three drunks were. Cliff got his flight back to London and Del and I caught our plane to Manchester. When we finally got on the plane the fellow who was sat next to us ordered a drink and when it came it was in a plastic cup. He was just about to take a drink when Del said, "You can't drink out of that cup," went into his bag and gave him a Waterford Crystal glass which we had been given at the Benson & Hedges tournament. The fellow looked shocked and said, "My word, you snooker players do live well."

When I had a contract with BCE, Dave Fisher, the governor, asked me to go to Japan to design a range of twelve cues for his company. So it was after a tournament in Australia that I flew on to Japan. I had talked Cliff Thorburn into coming over with me, although his air tickets were for him to fly back direct to Canada, and my manager Del Simmons came along, too. We had to get the Tube on arrival, which initially was a problem as we could not follow the Japanese signs and symbols. Eventually, by asking another Westerner, we managed to get off at the right station. I managed to sort all the cues out and we went back to Tokyo.

Later that day when I was in my room I suddenly heard the bottles in the fridge rattling. Then the windows also began to shake and soon I realised it was an earthquake. I just could not move my feet; the noise it was generating was terrifying. I was just stood there looking at the windows and waiting for them to fall in on me; how they stayed intact I do not know. When we met up afterwards Cliff, who happened to be in the shower at the time of the quake, said that when it was happening he didn't think he'd survive it. All he could think of was that when they found him they wouldn't have known who he was because he should not have been in Tokyo at all. The hotel we were in was built apparently to sway a certain distance when they had an earthquake. We were 50 miles away from the epicentre of the quake and there were 26 people killed by it. The morning after, when I was in bed, there were some strong aftershocks. I thought that it was starting all over again and felt sick from it. My stomach was churning over, as I was terrified we would have another quake just as strong.

The night after we were told to get a taxi to this bar in Tokyo. On the way I fell asleep and unknown to me Cliff and Del got the driver to stop and let them out. They then told him what to say and all I knew was the taxi driver woke me up saying, "Hiroshima 10,000 yen," and held his hand out for the money. I went into a right panic as the taxi driver was shouting louder and louder and virtually turned round in his seat to face me. I could not think what had happened; I could not even remember whether Del and Cliff had been with me. The one thing I did know was that I had no money with me and I just did not know what to say, I was absolutely terrified and puzzled. Del and Cliff let me suffer for about five minutes before they came back to the taxi laughing their heads off. I must say it was one of the best wind-ups I have ever had done to me, I was absolutely scared to death.

On the last night in Japan we were invited out for a meal with the governor of the cue company. There were four of us and we sat in a room of our own with the chef cooking the meal in front of us. When the chef got round to making the sweet, which he also made in our view, it took him about half an hour as he was throwing ingredients in the air and catching them, which made it into a real cabaret act. I will always remember that the cost of the sweet alone was the equivalent of £200. When watching the golf many years later I saw the governor of the cue company in Japan advertising the Big Bertha range of golf clubs, which he had opened in America.

In 1974 I was playing a week's exhibitions around the Norfolk area and the last one of these was at Sheringham Conservative Club. Before I left for the hotel I got a message to phone a Roger Lee who wanted to invite me to stay the night at his house instead of booking into a hotel. I arrived at his house, which was in Holt, and Roger had gone ahead to Sheringham Conservative Club to make sure that everything was ready for the evening, leaving his wife Lee to look after me. Well, I think she must have expected someone like Joe Davis with the act that she tried to put on - it was so false. She was trying to be on her best behaviour, saying things like, "Did you have a good journey? Would you like a drink of tea? Can I take your suitcase?" It was pathetic to listen to so I decided to end it by asking for some beans on toast. When she put them in front of me I took one bite of them and spit them out and said, "How can you make a fuck-up of beans on toast?" From then on every other word she used was the F-word. Roger arrived home at about 2pm and it turned out that it was Roger Lee of the Brother Lees, the singing comedy trio. We became very close friends, in fact I finished up going to stay the week with him before any big tournament I had to play in as he had his own table and I could get as much practice as I wanted without being disturbed. I am sure that it helped me with my performances in a lot of the East Anglian tournaments.

I was staying at his house one week when he was himself away, working for three nights in Hull. I could not believe it when he arrived home in the early hours of the morning, as he had said they would be staying in Hull. The second night I said to Lee that he obviously does not trust us, so we laid a single mattress out and put it in front of the fire with a blanket on, alongside two ash trays and two wine glasses with a little wine in each. I then put a note on the pillows reading "and you will never know", then we went to bed. Two weeks later I was playing in Carlisle and I phoned Margot at home and it was Roger Lee that answered the phone. All I got was "and you will never know" and he put the phone down. I do know one thing, we have been the closest of friends ever since.

OUT OF THE BLUE INTO THE BLACK

I think that one of the best clubs for me when I went playing exhibitions was without doubt the Victoria Club in Nottingham. It was a magnificent building and I hit it off with the owner George Aitkin straight away - probably the fact he was also a bookmaker with a chain of betting shops had something to do with it! He invited me to join a party of five to go and see the Arc de Triomphe horse race in Paris with everything paid for and a room in the George Cinq Hotel, which without a doubt was one of the nicest places I had ever stayed in and, I might add, the most expensive, too. The six of us had the whole of the east wing on the first floor to ourselves and we had a whale of a time there. I went to the Arc de Triomphe for the next six years with everything paid for by George Aitkin and we never saw a live race as we watched every race on the television in the bar at the racetrack. Then in the evening, it was a pub-crawl all over Paris. One year I had forgotten my passport but somehow he got me there and back without it.

He once phoned me to ask if I could get down to his club for 11 o'clock the following morning. When I arrived he took me up to his office and explained that we were going to go downstairs and have a nice lunch. He was waiting for someone else who would be there soon and shortly after that the phone rang with a message for him to come down to the restaurant. We went over to a table where a beautiful girl was sat. She was introduced to me as Penny Plummer from Australia and had just won the Miss World competition.

He also had a nightclub with strippers on where you could drink until 1 o'clock in the morning. The room next to the stripper's was always mine when I was playing exhibitions in the Nottingham area, so again I was saving money with no hotel bills to pay. The luckiest day of my life was during the early Seventies after I had completed a tour of North Wales in which I had played five snooker exhibitions. I set off on my way home and had just got on to the dual carriageway through Flint when I must have fallen asleep at the wheel. The car swerved across the road and was hit by a 20-ton lorry just behind the front offside door. It split the car in two and when I finally managed to get out of the car I could not believe that the only injury I had was a graze over my left eye. When I put my hand in my pockets they were both full of broken glass from the windows and windscreen. When I looked at the crash scene afterwards I saw it was the lorry that saved me as if it had not hit me I would have gone into a big concrete wall, which was directly in front of me. The only unfortunate thing was that my old number 35 cue had been in the back of the car and had been broken into four pieces, though of course it could have been much worse. Eventually the police arrived and sorted everything out before they phoned and got me a taxi to take me home. After we had been driving for about five minutes the taxi driver turned to me and said I was very lucky to be talking to him. When I asked him why, he said that he was the local undertaker and the taxi driving was only a part-time job! Either way, fate had played a hand in my meeting up with him through one means or another.

When I finally got home at about 4 o'clock in the morning Margot did not believe a word I said. She thought that I had hidden the car and that I had been playing cards in the casino in Manchester, so I had to show her all the broken glass in my pockets. A couple of days later a pal of mine, Cliff Curtis from Rileys Snooker, turned up to see if he could fix the cue back together as being a maple cue the breaks were pretty clean. He managed to get it back together again. Up until then I had a two-piece cue, which I used in my exhibitions, but as soon as he brought my old cue back to me I decided to try it and I must say it felt better than ever! You could have said that I was making the biggest breaks with a cue with the biggest breaks!

Chapter 11

Wind-Ups and Cock-Ups

Other Tournaments 1971-1981

I WAS well known on the circuit for my jokiness and for my wind-ups. I had the nickname 'Gentleman John' as I did not argue with the referees and always tried to give autographs and interviews after the tournaments. A lot of this changed when I got Myasthenia Gravis, as I would be too depressed to give many interviews, although I tried to cover up this fact as much as I could.

In 1978 the South African, Perrie Mans, beat me in the first round at the Crucible. Margot and I had gone up to the Embassy room and were having a drink. The closing captions were on the TV and they showed the arena before they zoomed in on an elderly man still in his seat, fast asleep. After the show ended, Nick Hunter, the BBC producer, came in and put his arm round me to say how sorry he was that I had been knocked out and without thinking I said, "I am a bit sick but the thing I did not like was the closing captions when they went to a close-up of my father asleep." I left it there and asked Nick if he wanted a drink so we sat down talking. He then mentioned my 'father' again, saying how sorry he was. I knew he was there for the taking so I got a message to David Vine

101

to let him in on the joke. Shortly after, I saw Nick look over my shoulder, and then say he would not be a minute. He went out of the door and David Vine asked Nick if he had heard what had happened with the closing captions, which Nick fell for hook, line and sinker. It was three weeks before he found out that it was not my father that they had shown asleep at the Crucible. Apparently, everywhere he worked after that, they pulled his leg about this.

The following day I was having a meal with Ted Lowe when one of the TV team came and asked me to be ready for the start of the Griffiths-Mountjoy match. I had been asked to give an interview to the Welsh TV crew and the match was due to start in about fifteen minutes' time. As soon as he had gone, Ted said to me, "It must be a wind-up, what can they want you to say about two Welshmen?" I was ready for whatever they had in store for me and sure enough they had one of the Welsh TV commentators at the table with a mike. He introduced me to the crowd and then turned to me and asked me the longest question I have ever heard - but in Welsh - so I pondered for a while and just replied, "No, I cannot agree with that." The crowd just fell apart, but he did not stop there and carried on with an even longer question in Welsh. Again I feigned deep thought for a while and replied, "Yes, I have to agree with you there," so after that he decided to give up as the crowd were now laughing their heads off.

At one of the tournaments when I was commentating, Ted Lowe and the director were having technical problems with the commentary. Just for fun I thought I would make a noise, which must have sounded just like a clock ticking. I did this for about a minute when on our earpieces we could hear that all hell had broken out in the director's cabin as they frantically looked for the clock that be could hear 'ticking' over the mike. Keith Phillips, the director, could be heard shouting, "Where is that fucking clock? Someone find it now!" However, I did not own up to making the noise as the director had got seriously wound up about it and it was causing them a few problems.

At another tournament, David Vine phoned me up and asked me to go down to the studio for a Christmas special that he had managed to get from the BBC. Of course, even though I had a good idea that it was a wind-up, I still had to go through with it, so off I went to the studio where David was sat there waiting for me. He told me that they had just got a half-hour slot over the Christmas period and started to fire questions at me, which I just answered without really thinking too much about what he had asked me. This went on for the full half hour. David then closed the programme, looked at me and said, "You thought that was a wind-up. Well it was not a wind-up and I will also add that it was the best interview you have ever done with me. I could not have done it any better if I had tried."

When he told me this I could not believe it. I did not remember any of the questions that he had asked me or the answers that I had given but when the programme went out I was very pleased with the outcome. I suppose I came over better thinking it was a wind-up as it made me more relaxed.

At the UK Championships at the Guildhall, Preston, it was an ongoing joke that every year Frank Baker, one of our security people, and his uncle who was general manager at the Guildhall, would catch me out with a wind-up. One year I decided I would get my own back on them and devised a wind-up with the help of the BBC make-up artist, Barry Hearn and his driver. I dressed up as an Arab sheikh and the idea was that I would turn up at the Guildhall to meet Barry Hearn, driven there in his limousine. Frank would be told that he was from Qatar and he wanted to see how they went about putting a snooker tournament on. We were going to get Frank to show him all round the Guildhall to see where everything was situated and eventually they would end up at the bar, where Frank and his uncle would have to act as bodyguards for the 'sheikh'. After getting a drink and talking to them he would throw some of his drink all over Frank, to which Barry would say, "Don't be offended, that means he likes you." Then we planned to spray his uncle with a soda siphon placed on the bar, and Barry would say, "He really likes you." But just as we were getting into the car to begin the trick, one of the BBC crew came up to me and said we couldn't carry on as someone had spoiled the wind-up and already told them. So all my efforts and planning were in vain for what could have been an excellent joke.

In May 1978 we were at Warner's Holiday Camp on Hayling Island. It had been arranged for me to play in a round-robin match in nearby Portsmouth. The Lord Mayor and civic dignitaries were all present when Ken Dawson, the referee and a very good friend of mine, announced to the audience that "John Spencer has won the break and will toss off" by mistake. So I made out that I was going to undo my trousers, saying, "I thought we were here to play snooker but I don't mind!" - much to the audience's delight. I just couldn't stop myself from saying things like that.

Chapter 12

The Snooker Stars

From Dracula to The Hurricane

Ray Reardon

IN THE early days of my professional career, most of my exhibitions were played with Ray Reardon. We always spent two weeks in Scotland every year playing on behalf of Rileys Snooker and were organised by a great friend of mine, Bob Bailey, the manager of Rileys Scotland. Everyone that saw us thought that we were the best of friends, which certainly was not true as far as I was concerned. In fact, I do not think that the two of us ever went out together socially throughout my professional career unless there was a third party with us.

In the late 1960s there was a rumour going round that I was being invited to go to Canada to play some exhibitions with Cliff Thorburn, then a few weeks later it was Reardon who was going. I found out that Jack Karnehm, the Chairman of the Billiards Association, had phoned Canada to say that I was unavailable and that Ray Reardon would go in my place. Reardon, who had cancelled all his exhibitions for the period he would have been in Canada, was left in the lurch when Canada cancelled the trip and I was delighted when I heard the news.

Another time I got a call from Bob Bailey to say that he had got the usual two weeks' bookings for us, though he went on to say that two of them had been arranged by Reardon. The best exhibition that we always had on these trips to Scotland was at Glasgow University where there would probably be a crowd of about 500 students shouting and cheering all through the match and the atmosphere was simply terrific.

We hardly ever stayed in the same hotel on these exhibitions, as Reardon always seemed to find someone who would let him stay at their house. It was the same if we went to any functions. After the exhibitions or functions he would not go talking to just anyone but instead always used to find out who organised the snooker bookings and that was who he would be with for the rest of the night. There was a couple in Bristol who he always stayed with when he was down that way and they invited me on a few occasions to stay with them. I knew I would have to play a few frames of snooker with their son if I did but as far as Reardon was concerned it was free lodgings for the night. The other thing I did not like about him was that he was the sort of person who could laugh 24 hours a day if it was to his advantage. The only two people whose houses I stayed at on the snooker circuit were Roger Lee and Ray Edmonds, as I could do anything I wanted to do without having to ask; in other words it was just like being at home.

John Pulman

John Pulman was the true professional that always gave his best and was never beaten until the winning line had been reached. The funniest moment I had with John was when we were in Australia. We had to go from Sydney to Newcastle to play an exhibition and when we got there we found the hotel we were staying at could only manage a twin-bedded room. It was a scorcher of a night and every window in the hotel was left wide open, so we unpacked and went downstairs and had a few drinks. We eventually went to bed but I could not get to sleep, it was just too hot. Then about 5 o'clock in the morning there was such a noise outside which turned out to be a delivery of beer. They were just throwing the metal barrels off the trailer and I could hear Pulman muttering to himself. The next moment he jumped out of bed and leant out of the window. He started screaming at the draymen and when I looked up I could not stop laughing as he had not got a stitch on and was leaning out of the window. Every time he shouted his balls were jumping up and down like a yo-yo, it was one of the funniest sights I have ever seen.

Graham Miles

Graham Miles had one of the most peculiar stances in the game with his cue just under his left ear when he was down on a shot. He was always on the last minute for everything. We used to hold a lot of our qualifiers for the various tournaments at Bristol and we had a rule that if you were more than ten minutes late to start your match you lost a frame. Graham holds a record with this by arriving forty minutes late and therefore forfeiting the first four frames, but lucky for Graham his opponent did not turn up at all so it went in the records that he had won 5-4 without even playing. Another time he was playing a match and cleared up with a great 36 break, only to hear the referee award the frame to his opponent who was 38 in front - Graham had gone in off the previous shot and he had forgotten about it.

Graham phoned me up in the mid-Eighties to see if I would play an exhibition with him in a circus ring in Great Yarmouth. He said that the circus ringmaster had come to him at the end of one of Graham's exhibitions to see if he could arrange this. The ringmaster obviously knew nothing about snooker exhibitions as he was talking about pushing the snooker table in to the ring with an elephant, but Graham said this was impossible. When they started talking about money, he agreed to all that Graham asked for, which to us seemed a little odd so we were not sure if we would be getting paid for the exhibition. Anyway, a few weeks later Graham and myself were stood in this circus ring with a full house of spectators who, once we had started, went quiet. All you could hear was the roar of the lions and tigers in the background. We finished the show with the trick shots and to our surprise he paid us our money.

About a month later I was driving into Manchester when I saw a sign, which had the circus ringmaster's name on it. This time he was doing bungee jumping at Heaton Park near Manchester, which is a bit different from snooker. There was no chance of me getting involved in that!

OUT OF THE BLUE INTO THE BLACK

Alex Higgins

When Alex first came to England he stayed with the Chairman of the Bolton Snooker League, Jim Worsley, who then started to arrange exhibition matches with Alex and myself all around the Bolton area. Alex was never a problem. One night we had just played an exhibition in Accrington and decided afterwards that we would go to a club for a drink. We were walking down the road when we saw a police car coming along and Alex just stepped out in front of it and stopped it. He walked round to the policeman and said, "I am Alex Higgins the snooker player. Can you run us to the nightclub?" As it happened the policeman really let fly at Alex and said what he would do for him if he ever did that again. But seriously, Alex really thought he should run us to the club. We went on as though nothing had happened but that gave me some idea of what to expect in the future.

After he beat me in the 1972 World Championship his manager arranged a money match with me at the Radcliffe Civic Hall for £1100. It would be a weeklong match, the best of seventy-three frames, which was 6 frames in the afternoon all week with 6 frames in the evening Monday to Friday, and then 7 frames on the Saturday evening. The referee was a 74-year-old man who had played in the Radcliffe league all his life.

As soon as we started the match Alex had made a break of 36, then went in off the blue and the referee shouted out, "36 to HIGGINS, foul stroke, 5 to JOHN." That went on for the whole week. The game went down to the 73rd frame and I managed to win it with a fluke. Alex went for a plant into the corner pocket and the reds went all over the table. A red just dropped into the middle pocket but the white finished tight on the baulk cushion and Alex tried to roll up behind the brown. He hit it a bit too hard and I cleared up with a 79 to win the match 37-36, but if that red had not gone into the middle pocket I would have had to play from off the baulk cushion with reds spread all over the table. It would have needed a miraculous shot from me to get it safe and Alex would have been big odds-on to win the frame and match. From then on, if my opponent got a fluke it never bothered me as in the long term only the winner can be lucky.

Alex probably had the quickest snooker brain in the game. It was very rare that he took the wrong shot. His speed was not in his cue action, but his actual speed around the table. Many a time I have seen him waiting for the white to stop to play his next shot, which was something that the crowds loved. Arriving so soon after *Pot Black* had started the ball rolling, I think that Alex did more for the game than any other player at that time. The one thing about him was that you never saw him play to anything but a full house and I cannot think of anyone else that could boast that except Jimmy White. Alex never had any problems getting exhibitions, as crowds would always flock to see him.

The one thing that he did not like doing was signing autographs after the match and this particular night when I had played him he turned up with a rubber stamp with his name in capital letters. He just sat there and stamped the autograph books as the fans all stayed in the line and thanked him for his autograph. Only Alex could do something like that and get away with it.

OUT OF THE BLUE INTO THE BLACK

During the interval at one of my exhibitions in Carlisle against Alex Higgins, who should walk in but the trainer of Highland Wedding, the 1969 Grand National winner, who took the horse up to the table to the cheers of the crowd. Within two minutes Alex had jumped on the table and onto the horse's back, which was shortly followed by the horse's tail lifting up. Then the biggest load of horseshit was spread all over the floor at the baulk end of the table. Immediately someone in the crowd shouted, "Wouldn't you if he jumped on your back?" and with that the crowd must have been laughing for about five minutes. The interval was extended while the mess was cleaned up and some sawdust put down, but after the interval any safety shots to the baulk end of the table really were safe. The smell was horrible so you had to play your shot pretty quickly and get away before you passed out.

At an exhibition that had been arranged for me to play Alex in Middlesbrough, I was in the hotel when I got a telephone call from the organiser to say that Alex had refused to play. Sure enough, when the evening papers came out the story said, 'Higgins refuses to play'. At about 6 o'clock the organiser came to my room and said, "We are all right, he's now agreed to play." I said to the organiser, "Well if he plays, I don't. After what he has done, the spectators shouldn't be treated like that." I said I would play an exhibition against seven of the club members, giving them 200 starts, and if they beat me I would forfeit my fee. The organisers said that anyone that did not want to stay could get their money back. They agreed to do this and when I got to the club they gave me a tremendous reception after I had explained why I had done this. Only two people left and got their money back. I was lucky Alex went home, as had he come to the club I was sure that the majority of the spectators would certainly have been on his side.

It was in 1976 that Embassy came into snooker and sponsored the World Championship. The first year it was split into two halves, the top half playing in Middlesbrough and the bottom half playing at Wythenshawe Forum, where the two winners were to also play the final. Ray Reardon won the Middlesbrough semi-final and Alex Higgins won the semi-final at Wythenshawe. Margot and myself went down to watch Alex play his semi and as we were there rather early we went into the office where all the Embassy girls stayed. As soon as they saw me they wanted to know what Alex was like as they had heard so much about him. I was trying to explain how he could be as nice as anyone, then for no reason at all he would blow his top, but I assured them that I was sure he would not be any trouble. After the evening session of the semi, Margot and myself finished up in the office talking to the Embassy girls when who should come in but Alex and another friend of mine, Henry West. They were having a right go at each other about a watch that Henry had and Alex was saying it was his. This was still going on when we left the office and just as I was going down the steps Alex for some reason started calling Margot all sorts of filthy names and that did it, I just blew my top. I ran up the steps and threw myself at Alex and we hit the office door and finished up on the floor with all the Embassy girls looking at us. Then in walked a policeman who apparently had been watching all that had been going on outside. He soon sorted us out and when he had gone the Embassy girls could not stop laughing and said that when the door burst open they thought Alex would be on top of me after what I had told them earlier.

It was in the early 70s that Alex went on a trip to India to play in a tournament and as soon as he got off the plane he took his shirt off. That was taboo in India so the officials told him to put it back on, which he refused to do. He was told that if he did not put it back on he would be sent on the next flight back to England, though he still would not give way to them and was subsequently sent home. That was how stubborn he could get at times when he was in the wrong mood.

I will never forget when Alex came to see me when I was first diagnosed with Myasthenia Gravis. That was the gentle, caring side that nobody ever saw of him.

Cliff Thorburn

Cliff Thorburn was otherwise known as 'The Grinder' because of the way he played his snooker - he never rushed around the table and was a very hard man to beat. When I think of the playing conditions in Canada it amazed me how he could adjust as well as he did to the conditions in Britain, where the tables were much slower and the pockets much smaller. In fact, had he come over to this country two or three years earlier and got used to the tables I am sure he would have won quite a few more tournaments than he did. He certainly was not the fastest of players but he was a player who very rarely played the wrong shot and he gave me a very hard battle when we met in the final of the 1977 World Championship, which was the first at the Crucible. He had a great temperament for the game and had nerves of steel; he was never bothered about taking the difficult shot on as long as the reward was there, should he get it, which I think is one of the main things when playing snooker.

In 1972, during one of my visits to Canada, I went to play an exhibition with Cliff in Edmonton. When I got to the club, Cliff was there and told me that his mate had arranged for two young ladies to come along and have a drink with us. The club was on the first floor and we just kept watching the stairs when two real beauties came up. Cliff and I looked at each other when two six-foot blokes came up behind them and went and sat with them. Shortly after, two very ordinary looking girls came up and went and sat down on their own, and they turned out to be the ones we were to have a drink with after the exhibition. Anyway, we started the exhibition match and Cliff potted a red at 100mph up the cushion and into the corner pocket. I said to him, "Who are you trying to impress?" at which point we both started laughing and all the audience joined in with us. After a few minutes the audience got fed up with it and finished up with a slow handclap, which managed to get Cliff and me back on our feet. The following night we were playing another exhibition in Edmonton and the sponsors for the night had put up $1,000 for the highest break. In the third frame Cliff made a 146 break, but in the very next frame I made a 147, which absolutely brought the house down. Everyone in the crowd was cheering and shouting - except for Cliff of, course. I am sure that this must be a record for two high breaks in consecutive frames.

Willie Thorne

Willie Thorne was one of the characters in the game who unfortunately never showed his snooker hall form when he was playing in a major tournament. I would say that the reason for this was that he was too aggressive when playing the game and took a lot of wrong shots. When Willie went into a major tournament he had to win every frame in one visit and certainly took far too many risky shots. Like me, Willie loved to have a gamble. When mobile phones first became more accessible - but long before their ascent into widespread popularity - Willie had one that seemed the size of a suitcase. He took it along whilst playing golf at St. Pierre Golf Course in Wales and he was on the ninth tee when his mobile phone rang. It was a mate of Willie's who had a tip on the horses. Of course, Willie couldn't refuse and had £400 on it. It lost - there was only Willie who could do that, lose £400 in the middle of a game of golf!

Eddie Charlton

Eddie Charlton, who was the oldest player on the circuit and probably the slowest too, made sure he did not take any chances in leaving his opponent with a rash shot. He was as dangerous as anyone and a very good break-builder when he got in. He did a lot of good for the game of snooker by putting on tournaments in

THE SNOOKER STARS

Australia and arranging exhibitions for English players. In fact, with the tournaments and the exhibitions he took me to Australia eleven times throughout my career. On one occasion I asked him to book us a holiday for myself and Margot, along with Del Simmons and his wife Audrey, Alex Higgins with his wife and baby Lauren, her nanny and their luggage, which consisted of Alex's eight suitcases. He booked us into a hotel in Suva on the island of Fiji. We arrived at Nadi airport and were put onto a bus to take us to Suva. The bus was a rickety old thing just like the ones in the *St Trinian's* films, with broken windows and without doors. The route was mountainous and one of the most frightening you could travel as we looked out of the windows close to sheer cliff edges.

When we arrived in Suva, Margot's first words were that it "smelled". We were shown to the hotel, which wasn't up to the standard we expected; "This is a good start to our holiday," I thought. Margot decided to go for a walk when she met an American lady whom she got talking to. She told Margot that Suva was on the rainy side of the island and that it had rained continuously for a week. So Margot came back to the hotel and cancelled our bookings and instead booked a flight back to Nadi for the eight of us that same day. She also booked us all into John Newcombe's tennis ranch at Nadi over the phone. We went to the local airport where there was just the one plane with a woman stood at the front of it, putting her make-up on. It turned out that she was the pilot!

Once we arrived back at Nadi we were transported via taxi to the hotel situated by the sea. As soon as we had settled in our rooms we went to the tennis courts where Alex and me decided we would have a tennis match. Alex could never play anything just for fun and he certainly could not play tennis. He finished up diving all over the place to try and get the ball back and this was on a concrete court. By the time we had finished he had cuts all over himself. On another evening we were all having a meal with an Australian wine, but Alex wouldn't drink anything other than French wine. So he drank alone and ended up drunk and, showing off, he jumped into the swimming pool. There was just one problem; he couldn't swim a stroke and shouted for help. We were in stitches laughing at him and just ignored him as we pretended to walk off, before we took pity on him and jumped in the pool to rescue him.

One boat trip took us to Castaway Island, which was a beautiful spot where we really enjoyed ourselves. Margot and Audrey decided to sunbathe on the beach and were lying on their fronts when a sidewinder snake went past them, bringing about a rather swift end to their sunbathing. We went back to the boat, which was small, only seating eight passengers, and set off in beautiful weather. However, once we were out at sea the weather changed and a spray started coming over us. As we sailed further away from the island it got worse and worse. Eventually we were panicking as we were getting soaked to the skin and the boat was being tossed all over the place. The pilot looked frightened himself. This went on for about half an hour and we thought we would never make it back to land, but by the time we arrived back at the shore there was not a ripple in the water. Eight people who looked frightened to death and were soaking wet lumbered back onto dry land in what was again calm and beautiful weather. I certainly did not ask Eddie to book me any more holidays!

Another time I got a phone call from Eddie to ask me if I could fly out again to Australia to arrive on the Saturday morning as he had got a TV slot for a match. I said that I would come out and Eddie arranged the flight for me. The only problem was that before I agreed I had forgotten I had a snooker exhibition in England on the Monday. So I flew out on the Saturday morning, played the TV show and then flew back on the Sunday. The following night I had to go and play the exhibition in Bolton for Jim Worsley and, halfway through the show, I actually fell asleep when I was down on a shot. Eventually we had to cancel the exhibition, as I could not keep my eyes open, I was absolutely shattered from that brief trip to Australia and the long hours in the air. I had to get someone to drive me home where I went straight to bed and slept for fourteen hours. It took me another couple of days before I was back to normal.

Kirk Stevens

Whenever we played a major snooker tournament there was always a few snooker groupies hanging around; the only trouble was they never hung around me, it was always Kirk Stevens that they made for! Oh, well... no accounting for taste. Kirk was without a doubt one of the nicest pros on the circuit, he would do anything to help you and was always so cheerful it was a pleasure to be in his company. When he went out to play he always wore his all-white dress-suit and looked immaculate. I never saw him have any trouble with anybody and then he showed what a great snooker player he was when he made the only 147 break in a televised Benson & Hedges tournament. I was very sorry when he decided to go back to Canada, as the game needed professionals like him.

Joe Johnson

The player that I had a lot of respect for in the Eighties was Joe Johnson, who came through as an unfancied and largely unheard of underdog and then went on to beat Steve Davis in the 1986 World Championship final. He than proved to everyone that it was no fluke when he again reached the final of the World Championship, this time to finish runner-up to Steve Davis. Joe has since had a rough time of things with his health, which included a heart bypass. But when I saw him at the parade of World Champions at the 2005 Embassy World Championship he was as cheerful as he always used to be. I must confess it was great to see him like that after what he has been through.

Chapter 13

Spitting My Dummy Out
& Big Bad Bernard

ONE YEAR at the Benson & Hedges tournament at the Wembley Conference Centre, after the final I finished up sitting next to Ann Yates, the WPBSA tournament director, with three of my friends. We'd all had a few drinks and when I looked down I noticed that Ann's room keys were on the chair next to her. So I got my keys out of my pocket and swapped them with hers. About an hour or so later she decided to go up to her room for the night. Within a couple of minutes she came down again and went to reception to get another set of keys. About half an hour later we all decided to go to bed and, as I had Ann's keys, I thought I would pay her a visit. As I opened the door she had just come into the room after having a shower and didn't have a stitch of clothing on. I have never seen anyone disappear behind the bedsheets as quickly as she did. I just went round and sat on the bed chatting to her as though nothing had happened - mind you, I had had quite a few drinks by this time.

A couple of weeks later Margot and I went down for a break to Roger Lee's in Norfolk. It turned out to be a great week, as Roger knew all the best places to go. When it was time to go home, I asked Roger if he had a newspaper. He brought out the *Express* and I looked at the racing pages to pick out four horses for £5 trebles and a £5 accumulator so I would have something to listen to and keep me interested on the way home. The first names that jumped out at me were Certainly John, followed by Castel Memories, Guiburn and Water Colour. I did not tell Margot, as she hated me gambling and didn't know about the bet.

We set off on our way home with my attention on the clock, as the results would come through every hour on the radio. Unfortunately we had missed the first one as we did not leave until after 2 o'clock, but at 3 o'clock the first result was given and Certainly John had won at 11-4. The next was at 4 o'clock and Castel Memories had won at 6-1. I was getting excited but I still did not tell Margot. Then the 5 o'clock report came and Water Colour had won at 7-2, so I pulled into the next services, got out my calculator and told Margot that we had already won over £600 from the three horses that had won. We would have to wait until we got home as they gave the next racing results out at five to seven, but I told her that if the last one won it would come to at least £4,000.

I kept pulling her leg about gambling, as she wanted me to stop at every motorway service station to check the result. I was eager to stop too but I was determined to show her that gambling can be exciting and told her I wouldn't be stopping until we got home, where we would get some fish and chips and listen to the results at 7 o'clock. When they came on I knew Guiburn was number 11 and, as soon as it was said the winner of the 1.55 was indeed number 11, I let out a scream and threw my chips up against the ceiling. Margot did not hear the horse's name because of my screaming and I also missed the price, so then I had to phone my pal in Nottingham to find out. He told me it had won at 10-1, which was better than I could ever have imagined. I immediately got out my calculator and worked it out at £10,215 plus 55p with the tax paid and when I looked at the paper again I suddenly realised that an apprentice had ridden all four horses. Why I picked them I will never know, though of course I was instantly drawn to Certainly John through sharing the same name. Shortly after that Roger came up to our house as he was doing a few shows around the Manchester area. He gave me a picture frame with the actual newspaper that I had picked the horses from, with "The Lucky Sod's Club" written on it. At the bottom of the frame he put the four horses' names and their prices and, thirty years later, I still have a framed copy of the *Daily Express* with those winning horses marked off.

Two weeks later I was playing an exhibition at Bernard Bennett's club in Southampton. Bernard mentioned the winnings and obviously thought I knew all about the horses and wanted me to go across the road and have a bet with him. I said I would come across with him as long as I could use his phone and put a bet on with Corals, which would stop me getting involved with readies. This was at the time that Corals had brought out a new bet on the dogs, which was called a 'Corella'. It consisted of the first four forecasts at a meeting or the last four forecasts, so I did a perm with them, which came to £16. Again my gambling luck was at a premium, as one came up which won me a total of £2,465. It was with these winnings that we opened our first snooker club in Bolton called Spennies, so I can confidently say that I finished well in front with Corals as we opened a new snooker club using their money. While my luck was up, Bernard's was down as he lost £20, so I gave him that as I would not have won anything but for him talking me into going across to the bookies. The funny thing about winning so much in two weeks was that I completely lost interest in betting for about six months after that and never had a penny on the horses.

Spennies was located on the top two floors of a three-storey building, with the bar and restaurant on the first floor and the disco on the second. When we took it over we bought nine snooker tables, which fitted perfectly on the second floor. The only problem we had was taking the slates of the tables up to the second floor as it needed six of us to carry each slate up, so it took us about a week to get them upstairs and assemble them. Margot's mother and father also came in with us and looked after the kitchen side of things and Stuart from the Jolly Carter pub took over as the manager.

I must confess everything took off a lot quicker than we ever imagined and within weeks we had enough snooker members to keep the upstairs busy virtually all day. Downstairs we were soon doing about fifteen barrels of beer a week, which was more than we ever expected. We had to employ more staff to cope. One of the things that we had not taken into account when we bought it was that the Bolton evening newspaper and its offices were virtually next door to us and we found we got a lot of our custom from them. On Friday and Saturday nights we used to have them queuing on the stairs waiting for someone to come out. This was also the time when the popular snack at lunchtime was Steak Canadians and it was not long before we were doing 1,600 barmcakes a week, and of course the more barmcakes that you bought, the cheaper you got them. In making the sandwiches, Margot's father could cut the boiled ham so thin that you could see through it!

On one occasion I followed a young woman up the stairs and, always being one for the ladies, I asked her what she was doing in a snooker club. She said she had come for a job that we had advertised. I just looked at her short skirt and long legs and said, "You've got the job love." I took her in the office and she started to work for us the following day. It was during this time that David Scott, who had worked with Billy Fury as his roadie, began to come into the Mealhouse Lane club and eventually started to work for us. When Margot and myself decided to separate in 1987, he later became Margot's partner and is still a very good friend of mine.

When we were in our first snooker club, we decided to have a pram race for charity. The charity we chose was the Variety Club of Great Britain Sunshine Coaches and we decided that we would race round all the pubs in the centre of Bolton collecting money and getting people to sponsor us. We asked the manager of the Morrison's store in Bolton if we could borrow the supermarket trolleys. On the day I dressed up as a baby with my baby's hat on, a dummy in my mouth and a towel round my waist for a nappy. The idea was that we raced from pub to pub but we had to have a drink in every pub. There were about fifty trolleys racing altogether and you can imagine that by the time we were halfway round we were half-cut and it took us longer and longer in each pub.

I started off first and was one of the last to come home, but it was a great fun day. All in all we collected enough money to buy two Variety Club Sunshine Coaches, which was far better than we ever expected. It was a really good day and a lot of fun. There were bodies all over the street with the prams that had tipped up, especially towards the end of the race when the drink was beginning to tell. A few months later we received an invitation to go to the Guildhall in London for a special lunch, which was to be hosted by Prince Charles and Princess Diana. Unfortunately I was unable to go as I was out of the country playing snooker, but Margot went with our club manager Stuart and said what a lovely day it had been.

One weekend in 1987 I had arranged to play a couple of exhibition games in Bert Demarco's club in Edinburgh. He had arranged for me to stay in a beautiful flat right in the middle of Princess Street without any cost, as it was a friend of his that owned it. I felt like a millionaire when I came out of it. On the second night of my exhibitions I got chatting to this young lady called Lillian and we seemed to get on very well together. She gave me her telephone number so that I could give her a ring and we could have a night out together the next time I was in Edinburgh. It turned out that nearly every time I went to Bert Demarco's I would arrange to see Lillian and go out and have a drink with her. She was the manageress of a ladies' clothes shop and had two children. She came up with the idea of going on a holiday to Orlando in

Florida for two weeks, which was one week in Orlando and the second week in a resort further south called Clearwater. I thought I would enjoy that as I had already been to Coca Beach a few years earlier and I liked it then and I would like to see what it was like a few years later.

While we were in Orlando we spent all our time in Disney World and Water World to see all the dolphins doing their tricks. It surprised me how much more there was going on compared to my previous visit. Her two children could not believe what they were seeing. Unfortunately, I could feel my depression worsening and we had one or two arguments as she was used to getting her own way, being the manageress of a clothes shop. On the day that we should have been moving to our second port of call in Clearwater we had another row. I just said to her that I was packing my things and getting the next plane to England. I explained to the authorities at the airport that it was Myasthenia Gravis that was sending me into a deep depression and was the reason for me leaving a week early. Lillian went on with the rest of the holiday with her children.

When I got home I felt terrible about what I had done but could not help myself. As soon as she got back I gave her a phone call and she said they had a terrific time and told me all the things they had done. A few weeks later I phoned her up and invited her down for the weekend to my bungalow, which she accepted, and on the Saturday night we went out for a meal with my wife Margot and her new partner David. Halfway through the meal I could tell things were not going to work out as Lillian tried to take the whole night over, she just liked to organise everything. The atmosphere was not very good between us so the following day when she was due to go home I took her to Bolton train station and put her on the train. That was the last I saw of her.

In 1985 we opened our second snooker club in Bolton with thirty-two tables, four of which were in private rooms. There was also a lovely bar and eating area. We had Grace Kennedy and Robert Windsor come up from London to open it for us and, on the day of the opening, it was one of the worst days, weather-wise, for somebody driving up from London. I am glad to say that they made it safely and just had time to go to the hotel to get changed. They were a great success on the opening night. There were quite a few celebrities there including Bernard Manning and Peter Dennis, an actor friend of ours who spent the whole night pretending to be a waiter and had all the guests in stitches with his antics.

On Sunday afternoons we used to have a handicap competition for all the club members in which we would charge an entry prize and give out the money to winners of the handicap. Every now and then we would have a special one in which we would give out one of my trophies that had I won in the professional game. Although they were not like the trophies that you see today, our customers used to love winning them and that is why I only have one trophy left in the house, the Benson & Hedges Irish Masters, a cut-glass trophy, which I would never give away. Even with all those snooker tables in the club we always had quite a long waiting list of people who wanted to play, it was certainly a lovely sight when I walked into the club.